CREATED TO LEAD

*HOW YOU CAN BE
AN EXCELLENT LEADER*

RICHMOND DONKOR

Copyright © 2016 Richmond Donkor

All rights reserved. No part of this book may be reproduced, stored in a retrieval system, or transmitted in any form or by any means, electronic, mechanical, photocopying, recording, scanning, or otherwise, without the prior written permission of the publisher.

Cover design by: Hemant Lal
Layout & Formatting by: Hemant Lal
hlal@AaronProductionsIndia.com

Scripture quotations marked (CEV) are taken from the Contemporary English Version®. Copyright © 1995 American Bible Society. All rights reserved.

Scripture quotations marked (ESV) are taken from The ESV® Bible (The Holy Bible, English Standard Version®) copyright © 2001 by Crossway, a publishing ministry of Good News Publishers. ESV® Text Edition: 2011. The ESV® text has been reproduced in cooperation with and by permission of Good News Publishers. Unauthorized reproduction of this publication is prohibited. Used by permission. All rights reserved.

Scripture quotations marked (HCSB) are taken from the Holman Christian Standard Bible®, Copyright © 1999, 2000, 2002, 2003, 2009 by Holman Bible Publishers. Used by permission. Holman Christian Standard Bible®, Holman CSB®, and HCSB® are federally registered trademarks of Holman Bible Publishers.

Scripture quotations marked (KJV) are taken from the King James Bible. Accessed on Bible Gateway. www.BibleGateway.com.

Scripture quotations marked (NASB) are taken from the New American Standard Bible ® (NASB), copyright © 1960, 1962, 1963, 1968, 1971, 1972, 1973, 1975, 1977, 1995 by The Lockman Foundation. Used by permission. www.Lockman.org.

Scripture quotations marked (NET) are taken from the NET Bible® copyright ©1996-2016 by Biblical Studies Press, L.L.C. All rights reserved.

Scripture quotations marked (NIV) are taken from the Holy Bible, New International Version. Copyright © 1973, 1978, 1984, 2011 by Biblica, Inc.® Used by permission. All rights reserved worldwide.

Scripture quotations marked (NKJV) are taken from the New King James Version®. Copyright © 1982 by Thomas Nelson, Inc. Used by permission. All rights reserved.

Scripture quotations marked (RSV) are taken from the Revised Standard Version of the Bible, copyright © 1946, 1952, and 1971 the Division of Christian Education of the National Council of the Churches of Christ in the United States of America. Used by permission. All rights reserved.

All emphasis in Scripture quotations is added by the author.

Table of Contents

TRUE LEADERSHIP	6
THE FUNDAMENTALS OF LEADERSHIP	10
LEADERSHIP IN ACTION	19
VISION IN LEADERSHIP	25
DIVISION OF LABOR	36
THE CHARACTER OF A LEADER	48
GROWING YOUR LEADERSHIP SKILLS	65
TEAMWORK	78
THE BEST LEADERSHIP MODEL	89
LEADING TO GROW	100
REFERENCES	102
APPENDIX	113

TRUE LEADERSHIP

Leadership plays a vital role in our lives—which is why God instituted leadership from the very beginning. He expects mankind to be responsible with His creation and to take good care of it. Leaders are essential in an organization, a community, a family, and a nation. Leaders initiate action; motivate; provide guidance; and set an example for others to follow. They also coordinate with others in order to complete a task.

You may think you don't have leadership qualities based on your previous experience; your current condition; or what others think of you. However, the truth is that leadership is a gift, and at the same time it can be learned and taught. You can be trained to be a great leader. Every institution needs a leader to empower people to achieve their organization's goals. There are many leaders who care more about the power they possess than taking care of those under their leadership. The book of Isaiah says:

> You leaders of Israel should be watchdogs, protecting my people. But you can't see a thing, and you never warn them. Dozing and daydreaming are all you ever do. **11** You stupid leaders are a pack of hungry and greedy dogs that never get enough. You are shepherds who mistreat your own sheep for selfish gain. — Isaiah 56:10–11 (CEV)

Not everyone who holds a leadership position is truly a leader. Some are elected by popularity while others volunteer or are asked to fill that position. It is frustrating to find a church that is eager to follow a leader, yet does not have clear goals in place. The business sector regularly provides leadership training to its staff to enable them to be strengthened in the positions they hold. Businesses will evaluate themselves from time to time to see if they are being successful in moving toward their goals. If their goals are not being accomplished, they will implement new strategies to get back in alignment with their mission.

The Bible gives us examples of different kinds of leaders—some are good and some are bad. What does a good leader look like? What characteristics do they possess?

Good leaders are made, not born. If you have the desire and will power, you can become an effective leader. When God called Gideon, he told God:

> "Pardon me, my lord," Gideon replied, "but how can I save Israel? My clan is the weakest in Manasseh, and I am the least in my family." **16** The LORD answered, "I will be with you, and you will strike down all the Midianites, leaving none alive." — Judges 6:15–16 (NIV)

Another example is the call of Jeremiah:

> The word of the Lord came to me, saying, **5** 'Before I formed you in the womb I knew you, before you were born I set you apart; I appointed you as a prophet to the nations." **6** "Alas, Sovereign Lord," I said, "I do not know how to speak; I am too young." **7** But the LORD said to me, "Do not say, 'I am too young.' You must go to everyone I send you to and say whatever I command you. **8** Do not be afraid of them, for I am with you and will rescue you," declares the LORD. **9** Then the Lord reached out his hand and touched my mouth and said to me, "I have put my words in your mouth. **10** See, today I appoint you over nations and kingdoms to uproot and tear down, to destroy and overthrow, to build and to plant. — Jeremiah 1:4–10 (NIV)

A third example is the call of David:

> Now, LORD my God, you have made your servant king in place of my father David. But I am only a little child do not know how to carry out my duties. — 1 Kings 3:7 (NIV)

King Saul was told that he was going to be a king, this what he said,

> Saul answered, "But am I not a Benjamite, from the smallest tribe of Israel, and is not my clan the least of all the clans of the tribe of Benjamin? Why do you say such a thing to me?" — 1 Samuel 9:21 (NIV)

God saw something in each one of them, but they were blinded by their excuses. Good leaders are developed through a continual process of self-study, education, training, and experience. You will not be an effective leader without sufficient preparation. The skills required to be a good leader will be obtained through hard work and a willingness to learn. Leadership is a skill you will always be refining throughout your journey as a leader.

You must have an honest understanding of who you are, what you know, and what you can do. This book will elaborate on what makes someone a great leader, as well as other leadership principles. The information in this book will help anyone develop their leadership abilities so they can lead with power, confidence, and integrity.

CHAPTER ONE

THE FUNDAMENTALS OF LEADERSHIP

The word 'leader' typically makes someone think about a person with special abilities, charisma, and a strong personality. Many people may not accept a leadership position because it always comes with a lot of responsibilities. It is true that there are some people with a special gift to lead. However, everybody has the capacity to develop leadership qualities. When God called Moses to lead the Israelites, Moses was concerned that he didn't have the special abilities required to lead the Lord's people to freedom (Exodus 3:11). God told him in verse 12, "I will go with you."

Secondly, Moses expressed to God that he didn't know enough about Him to carry out the task. We may feel we don't know much about where the Lord wants us to lead—or we may feel unprepared for the job. However, God reminded Moses that he would not be alone and he would have the sufficient help of the One who is called "I AM." God beckoned him into obedience so Moses could discover more about who He is as they worked together to deliver the Israelites.

Thirdly, Moses was worried people would think he was lying about his encounter with God and would not believe that he was truly sent by Him (Exodus 4:1-9). Sometimes you will likewise feel that the people you are going to lead are more educated, richer, and more intelligent than you.

Moses' final excuse was that he did not have the ability to speak clearly (Exodus 4:10-17). It is not specified in the Bible what kind of difficulty Moses had with speech—whether he stuttered, answered slowly, or pronounced his words differently. Regardless of the nature of his speech impediment, God told Moses that it would not hinder him because God created his mouth and his mind.[1]

You may also feel, as Moses did, that you are not a good speaker. However, God saw what was in Moses, and because of that He didn't listen to the excuses of Moses. God guided Moses and helped him in every step of his journey. One thing I have observed when it comes to leadership is that you will never be ready unless you take the first step forward. With the help of God, you can be sure that you can do it.

The concept of leadership started when God was about to create the first human being. God said:

> Let us make mankind in our image, in our likeness, so that they may rule over the fish in the sea and the birds in the sky, over the livestock and all the wild animals, and over all the creatures that move along the ground. — Genesis 1:26 (NIV)

In this scripture, God was the coordinator before man was created. The Bible says:

> God created mankind in his own image, in the image of God he created them; male and female he created them. **28** God blessed them and said to them, "Be fruitful and increase in number; fill the earth and subdue it. Rule over the fish in the sea and the birds in the sky and over every living creature that moves on the ground." **29** Then God said, "I give you every seed-bearing plant on the face of the whole earth and every tree that has fruit with seed in it. They will be yours for food. **30** And to all the beasts of the earth and all the birds in the sky and all the creatures that move along the ground—everything that has the breath

of life in it—I give every green plant for food."
And it was so. — Genesis 1:27–30 (NIV)

God established leadership principles in these verses from the beginning. He planned, coordinated, delegated, blessed, and challenged humankind to multiply, and He gave them everything they needed to succeed in life.

In Genesis 2:15, "The LORD God took the man and put him in the Garden of Eden to work it and take care of it" (NIV). God started mentoring Adam and gave him specific instructions to follow:

> And the LORD God commanded the man, "You are free to eat from any tree in the garden; **17** but you must not eat from the tree of the knowledge of good and evil, for when you eat from it you will certainly die." — Genesis 2:16–17 (NIV)

Adam taught Eve what God told him from the beginning, and Eve was able to quote it to the serpent:

> The woman said to the serpent, "We may eat fruit from the trees in the garden, but God did say, 'You must not eat fruit from the tree that is in the middle of the garden, and you must not touch it, or you will die.'" — Genesis 3:2–3 (NIV)

God continued to follow up with them to make sure everything was going well, and He found that they had disobeyed Him:

> Then the man and his wife heard the sound of the LORD God as he was walking in the garden in the cool of the day, and they hid from the LORD God among the trees of the garden. **9** But the LORD God called to the man, "Where are you?" — Genesis 3:8–9 (NIV)

When they disobeyed God, they were disciplined and God sent them out of the garden of Eden.

Dr. Willis and Esmie Newman note that in His relationship with Adam, the Lord demonstrated several key leadership elements, including "vision, purpose, action, communication, problem solving, and delegation."[2] Dr. Richard J. Krejcir describes leadership this way:

> A basic description of leadership is the duty and call of the person who is in charge to take charge with courage and character, and to risk leading his/her people where they need to go and how they need to be led. It is a position that seeks vision, opportunities, and needs and then motivates others to get it done through the resources, talents, and time they can contribute.[3]

Leadership, in short, is one person's ability to influence other people positively. God moved or influenced the Trinity as a whole in the creation of human beings; and Adam influenced Eve by informing her about God's instruction to him. God provided everything for human beings to be successful—but men chose to disobey God's instruction. As a leader, you may also give instructions, but some will still choose to do what they want to do. Don't let this deter you from leading. Adam later learned a lesson and began to take his responsibilities seriously. Leadership can be learned and improved as time goes on.

The Bible describes many effective leaders, and each of them mastered what they did according to the vision and the challenge they were facing in their time and place. As a leader, you can learn valuable lessons from several biblical figures. For instance, Brooks Faulkner points out how a number of leaders in the Bible maintained effective attitudes toward the tasks they were called to accomplish:[4]

> **Paul: "Believe in something bigger than yourself."**
>
> "I have appointed you to be a light for the Gentiles, to bring salvation to the ends of the earth" (Acts 13:47 NET). ... He was thoroughly subservient to the will of God, and he was committed to a specific, meaningful mission. ...
>
> **Nehemiah: "Build on what God has given you."**

...God has given each leader specific gifts. Some are not as visible; all are useful.

Barnabas: "Bridge the gaps of differing opinions."

He was nicknamed "son of encouragement" (Acts 4:36 NIV). He bridged the gaps between the Greek and Jewish worlds. ...

Moses: "Blind your eyes to petty criticism."

Moses was seen as the patient leader of a people with little faith (Exodus 16:8, 16–20). ...

Elijah: "Bind the ties of love and courage."

...He loved God. He had the courage to speak to the evils of his day. "Where is your God?" he asked. "Perhaps he's sleeping and will wake up!" (1 Kings 18:27 HCSB). ... Effective leaders have the courage to speak even when it is unpopular to speak because they speak the truth with love.

Peter: "Bounce back after you are knocked down."

In Matthew 16, Peter was both a "rock" and a "stumbling block." ... Discouraged by the disapproval of Jesus, yet blessed by the warmth and affection of Jesus. Resilience may be the cornerstone of effective leadership.

Of course, God is the ultimate leader, as we see from the book of Genesis. One writer observes:

> The church exists for us to be in Christ our Lord, to be His people, His hands, and His feet. It started with the promise to Abraham and continues through us today. The covenant to Abraham represents one of the main themes of the Bible—that God fills and blesses us and we are called to share it as the primary purpose for our existence; we are blessed to be a blessing. The church is born and continues to live by the people God chooses, and the response we give. *"I will be your God and you will be my people"* is the relationship God calls us to—first to Himself and then to others. God is our God and we are called to be His people, so let's do this![5]

It should come as no surprise, then, that Jesus wants to establish His church on a strong and solid rock—which is a faithful and dependable leader:

> And I say also unto thee, That thou art Peter, and upon this rock I will build my church; and the gates of hell shall not prevail against it. **19** And I

> will give unto thee the keys of the kingdom of heaven: and whatsoever thou shalt bind on earth shall be bound in heaven: and whatsoever thou shalt loose on earth shall be loosed in heaven. — Matthew 16:18–19 (KJV)

Given this weighty responsibility, it's saddening that many church leaders are seeking material gain rather than seeking first the Kingdom of God. However, if we follow Jesus' instruction and we allow Him to use us, we will see a great revival in churches again. Jesus called the disciples from different professions and backgrounds, but He trained them and they became highly effective. The rest of the chapters in this book will discuss more about what will help you to discover and activate the leadership qualities within you.

CHAPTER TWO

LEADERSHIP IN ACTION

The basic definition of 'leadership' we found exemplified in the book of Genesis is "an ability to influence others for the better." Leaders must influence their followers positively so the latter will be able to stand on their own. In the context of a church, a spiritual leader is to direct people toward God's agenda. This is what God told Moses:

> Now go to the king! I am sending you to lead my people out of his country. — Exodus 3:10 (CEV)

> The LORD sent Moses with this message for the

king of Egypt: The LORD God of the Hebrews commands you to let his people go, so they can worship him. — Exodus 9:1 (CEV)

A spiritual leader's task is to move people from where they are to where God wants them to be. Once God's leaders understand His will, they will make every effort to pursue His purposes. The number one reason why pastors leave the ministry today is because they believe God has given them a vision for the church, but the people are not willing to go there. Encouraging people to move towards a goal will be challenging—that is why an effective leader must rely upon God's leading.

The greatest obstacle to effective spiritual leadership is pursuing your own plans instead of seeking God's will. God's concern is not to achieve or advance your dream or goal, but rather to turn His people away from self-centeredness and sinful desires and toward a relationship with Him. As effective spiritual leaders, it is our God-given responsibility to do everything we can to follow God's agenda.

Moreover, spiritual leaders must lead their followers to spiritual maturity. We can take people to places they have never been before. When they mature, they will be able to live an independent spiritual life.

Another important responsibility a leader should take into consideration is leading others to lead. Many of our leaders are so focused on the duties of their position that they overlook opportunities to delegate responsibilities to others. Leaders need to mentor others who will be able to carry on the work in the future. If we do not train others today to lead, our church or organization will not have leaders for tomorrow.

Spiritual leadership and leadership in general share many of the same principles. For instance, the most effective leaders are those who lead by example in every aspect of their life. The apostle Paul told Timothy:

> Let no man despise thy youth; but be thou an example of the believers, in word, in conversation, in charity, in spirit, in faith, in purity. — 1 Timothy 4:12 (KJV)

A leader must act in such a way that they will be respected in spite of their age, experience, or social status. Their life should become a pattern for their followers. If you're a leader, then, you should be careful to evaluate what example you are setting in your choice of words, in the types of conversation you engage in, in expressions of charity (love), in your enthusiasm for God and use of your spiritual gifts, in faith and integrity, and in maintaining the purity of your body.[6] As the apostle Paul said:

> In everything set them an example by doing what is good. In your teaching show integrity, seriousness... — Titus 2:7 (NIV)

John Gill's commentary on this scripture observes, "This means that it is not enough to merely say the right words. Your whole life should reflect the good works you are called to. You are to be a good example in every aspect of your life for those who follow you."[7]

To lead also means you need to see things other people aren't willing to see yet. Sometimes you will have followers who do not see what is really happening. You must have the wisdom and insight to lead your followers out of ignorance.

As a leader you are called to do the right thing even if people don't like the decisions you make. Do not allow fear of disapproval to keep you from making the difficult, necessary decisions. You can do the right thing with love because you know it will ultimately be the best for those in your care. It is your job to love in this way even if your followers do not reciprocate. Do what needs to be done, in the most beneficial way.

Moreover, you have to love and believe in what you are doing. When people see your passion and faith in the vision, they will willingly follow your direction.

Whatever we do in life, love plays a vital role. You can't lead if you don't have love in your life. The Bible says "If I give all I possess to the poor and give over my body to hardship that I may boast, but do not have love, I gain nothing" (1 Corinthians 13:3 NIV). Leading people involves a lot of energy, resource, time, and sacrifice. If you don't have love for God, people, and what you are doing, you will burn out.

So, what is love?

> Love is patient, love is kind. It does not envy, it does not boast, it is not proud. **5** It does not dishonor others, it is not self-seeking, it is not easily angered, it keeps no record of wrongs. **6** Love does not delight in evil but rejoices with the truth. **7** It always protects, always trusts, always hopes, always perseveres. **8** Love never fails. — 1 Corinthians 13:4–8 (NIV)

As Dr. Richard Krejcir explains in "Fruit of the Spirit Is Love," leaders who love will do what is best for others even if they are unappreciated and receive nothing in return. Love lives out what God's Word says even if it is difficult. It is not just a feeling—it is how we live our lives.

Ask yourself these questions on a regular basis to evaluate if you are living your life with God's love:

- In what ways is love revealed in the way I live my life?
- What can I do to develop a more loving attitude? What hinders me from living with love?
- How can I make love function better, stronger, and faster—even in times of uncertainty and stress?

God is the ultimate example of love. We must receive love from Him so that it can flow out of our lives. God's love is selfless, and it will mark our lives with selflessness. If you are implementing something for selfish gain, it is not love. Jesus gave up His life for us—this is true love.[8]

CHAPTER 3

VISION IN LEADERSHIP

To be able to lead successfully, love is vital, but you also need a vision. The Bible says in Proverbs 29:18, "Where there is no vision, the people perish…" (KJV). You will not be an effective leader if you do not have a clear vision—that reflects God and His Word.

The vision of a leader focuses on the future—it is a source of inspiration and motivation. It is the area in which the leader hopes to bring about change in an organization or in society. As a leader, you want your vision statement to outline where you want the group to be. It communicates both the purpose and values of your business or organization. It also answers the question, "Where do you aim to be?" It gives specific details of what your goals are for the future. It inspires you to give your best. It shapes your understanding, and serves as a light to help you see the way forward. For instance, when we look at the vision of Jesus Christ, it is very clear:

> The Spirit of the Lord is on me, because he has anointed me to proclaim good news to the poor. He has sent me to proclaim freedom for the prisoners and recovery of sight for the blind, to set the oppressed free, **19** to proclaim the year of the Lord's favor. — Luke 4:18–19 (NIV)

Jesus had this vision statement from the beginning, and when He started His ministry, He fulfilled His goal completely.

When you're developing a vision statement, make sure it addresses these questions:[9]

- What do we want to do going forward?
- When do we want to do it?
- How do we want to do it?

Your vision statement should be clear, hopeful, memorable, and realistic.[10] When God called Moses, He made the vision very clear to him. God specified the reason why He was sending him, and the message Moses needed to tell the Israelites and Pharaoh:

> The LORD said, "I have indeed seen the misery of my people in Egypt. I have heard them crying out because of their slave drivers, and I am concerned about their suffering. **8** *So I have come down to rescue them from the hand of the Egyptians and to bring them up out of that land into a good and*

spacious land, a land flowing with milk and honey — the home of the Canaanites, Hittites, Amorites, Perizzites, Hivites and Jebusites. **9** And now the cry of the Israelites has reached me, and I have seen the way the Egyptians are oppressing them. **10** So now, go. I am sending you to Pharaoh to bring my people the Israelites out of Egypt." — Exodus 3:7–10 (NIV)

Then the LORD said to Moses, "Go to Pharaoh and say to him, 'This is what the LORD says: Let my people go, so that they may worship me.'" — Exodus 8:1 (NIV)

There were three goals God had in mind when He decided to send Moses:

1. He wanted the Israelites to be free from slavery.
2. He wanted them to worship and develop a strong relationship with Him.
3. He wanted them to enjoy the promised land of plenty.

The condition of the Israelites was not what God had intended for them. They were worshiping false gods, from which God wanted to rescue them. Similarly, Paul said:

For he has rescued us from the dominion of darkness and brought us into the kingdom of the

> Son he loves, **14** in whom we have redemption, the forgiveness of sins. —Colossians 1:13-14 (NIV)

With this in mind, as a leader in a church, your vision should be in line with God's vision. Jesus said in the book of John 6:38–39:

> For I have come down from heaven not to do my will but to do the will of him who sent me. **39** And this is the will of him who sent me that I shall lose none of all those he has given me, but raise them up at the last day. **40** For my Father's will is that everyone who looks to the Son and believes in him shall have eternal life, and I will raise them up at the last day. — John 6:38–40 (NIV)

God will give people the freedom to serve and worship Him. The vision of a church is about God and the sheep that He has entrusted into your hands. It should focus on rescuing people from bondage and leading them to God—which means you can't do it alone or accomplish the vision without help. God called Moses and his brother to deliver the Israelites from the Egyptians, while He used Joshua to lead the people into the Promised Land.

Vision is crucial to the growth of a church or organization—it is the future picture of what your mission will lead to.

Some organizations and leaders struggle with what it means to have a vision. David Goetz notes about a study of pastors who were removed from leadership that "conflicting visions for the church was their greatest source of tension and the top reason they were terminated or forced to resign." It is clear that vision plays a crucial role in the success of a leader.[11]

The Benefits of a Vision[12]

A vision encourages unity. When a ministry or organization has a vision, it brings people together and involves everyone. It gives people the opportunity to have a clear picture of where the organization is headed so that they can choose if they want to be a part of it. When your church has a clearly communicated direction, you know that everyone involved wants to be there because they care about the vision. This in turn fosters unity, as everyone works together to reach that goal. The Bible says:

> It takes many parts to make a single body. **21** That's why the eyes cannot say they don't need the hands. That's also why the head cannot say it doesn't need the feet. **22** In fact, we cannot get along without the parts of the body that seem to be the weakest. — 1 Corinthians 12:20–22 (CEV)

A vision inspires people to action. A leader with a vision is inspiring and highly motivating. By contrast, a lack of vision can lead to apathy and stagnation. An example of this is in the book of Nehemiah. The people of Israel lacked the motivation to do anything for the city ruins in Jerusalem. However, Nehemiah was compelled by a vision to see the gates and wall of his city restored. When he brought this vision to the people, it inspired them to action. A leader with a vision from God will see their followers filled with excitement and a readiness to do the things of God.

An inspiring vision helps people feel like they are living a meaningful life. When people are participating in the vision of God, it makes them feel like they are a part of something bigger than themselves. A congregation that is actively involved in living out the vision is more likely to see themselves as a vital part of advancing God's Kingdom in the world.

A vision encourages leaders and organizations to be bold and take risks. Having a vision will oftentimes means going to new places and trying new methods. This provides the leadership and members many opportunities to be bold and take risks. Trying new things is not always effective—you have to encourage your congregation to continue to step out in faith until you find what works. As you all grow in boldness, it will be a testimony to the glory of God as more people are reached with His message. Taking bold steps of faith may come with the opportunity for big failure, but God is greater than even the most significant failures! The early churches were willing to risk their lives because of their clear vision.

A vision gives strength to leadership. A person with a strong vision will naturally find that people rally behind them. If you do not have a vision, you are merely wandering aimlessly, and your ability to lead will be hindered. A vision gives you clear direction so that you know where you are going. As you walk confidently in that direction, others will want to join you. This is the example that Jesus and His disciples left for us. Godly leaders will reflect the fruit of the spirit found in Galatians 5:22-23:

> But the fruit of the Spirit is love, joy, peace, forbearance, kindness, goodness, faithfulness, **23** gentleness and self-control. Against such things there is no law. (NIV)

When you have a vision and also walk in the fruit of the spirit, you will be strengthened in your role and find that people are eager to follow you.

A vision holds an organization to a standard of excellence. God reveals in His Word that it is important for us to do our work according to a high standard. We are called to do everything with excellence. We should not cut corners or be lazy in our efforts. In the Old Testament God required that people give their best when they brought animals for sacrifice (Leviticus 22:20–22). This was excellence in worship. In the New Testament Paul explains that God expects us to put forth our best efforts in our work. He says to perform as if we are working for him (Ephesians 6:5–8; Colossians 3:23–24). This is excellence in the marketplace.

When a group has a clear vision to follow, it encourages them to rise to excellence. People who play a vital role in accomplishing a task will be more likely to do their part with excellence. The vision itself tells people what standard they are supposed to strive for. With a solid vision in place, everyone will be able to evaluate if what they are doing is in alignment with the vision.

A vision sustains leaders and organizations through difficult challenges. People in ministry face many setbacks and difficulties. It is easy to experience discouragement and burnout. After all, it is not beyond the enemy to incite persecution against Christ's church (Acts 8:1). Spiritual warfare comes with the ministry territory (Ephesians 6:10–18). However, despite all of the things that come against Christians, they are able to continue forward and prevail. A strong vision can strengthen believers to persevere when they feel like giving up. It is a reminder of the reason they are enduring hardship, and a promise of what will come. Keeping the vision at the forefront of our minds can sustain us in our difficulties.

Do not be in a hurry to accomplish your entire vision in a short time. The book of Habakkuk 2:2–3 says:

> And the LORD answered me: "Write the vision; make it plain on tablets, so he may run who reads it. **3** For still the vision awaits its appointed time; it hastens to the end—it will not lie. If it seems slow, wait for it; it will surely come; it will not delay." (ESV)

Vision is the vehicle that carries leaders through the daily habits and challenges that build their church or organization and reach the world.

Leadership on a Mission

A vision talks about the future, but a mission statement talks about how to get from the present to that future goal. The mission of a leader or organization explains how you will get to where you want to be. It tells you what you are doing and why you are doing it. It serves as a guide that helps you make decisions every step of the way. A mission statement helps everyone stay united in their purpose so they can work together to reach their goal.[13]

In church, the mission will be daily, weekly, and monthly activities done in order to reach the church's vision. This is where most churches have failed because most of their activities are just following the pattern set by other groups, rather than being specific to their distinct vision. As a leader, if you don't have a clear mission, you will accept anything in your church or organization, which could lead to destruction.

For instance, all born-again churches are serving the same God, but each church has its own challenges according to its size, its location, and the vision of the church. This means your success in your previous church does not guarantee your success in your current position. Those who serve God should prioritize learning more about where God is leading them and the challenges the local people are facing.

The apostle Paul exemplified this principle when he wrote different letters to each of the various local churches. Even though the letters have some common themes, they each address different challenges the churches were facing because of their size, location, and vision. The letters are Romans, 1 Corinthians, 2 Corinthians, Galatians, Ephesians, Philippians, Colossians, 1 Thessalonians, and 2 Thessalonians. Another example of this principle is in Revelation 2–3: the apostle John described seven churches that each faced different shortcomings and challenges.

The mission of a church is clearly described in the Bible. According to one writer, the church is here for these purposes:[14]

- To preach the gospel
- To provide a spiritual atmosphere
- To reproduce the character of Christ

If our mission and the programs we do are designed to address the needs of the people, we will definitely see the fruit of our labor. The mission should help build people up. In the church, the most common programs are prayer meetings, Bible studies, seminars, and conferences. It is not wrong to copy other church programs. However, the danger is that if you don't give the right food to the sheep at the right time, it will not be helpful.

It is important to have a mission statement because it sets a course for your church or organization to reach its goals. It helps a group make decisions by reminding them what their purpose is. A mission statement also lets your team know what needs to stay the same and what needs to change. Furthermore, it helps you measure your current success in fulfilling your vision. Be sure that everyone on your team has a clear understanding of the missions statement, and regularly evaluate if you are where you want to be with respect to your mission.

As a church or other type of organization, you should do what you do because it makes an impact on the membership and it glorifies God— not because it's what every other group is doing. There is a saying, "You have to cut your jacket according to your size." If your organization is new, the need is different from an old organization.

Also, you should consider the demographics of your organization. Take into consideration how many women, men, children, employed versus unemployed people, and students you have. Is your membership multicultural? What are the immediate needs of the organization? What makes you unique?

All of these suggestions will help you write a great mission statement that will guide you towards fulfilling the vision of the organization. It is easy to copy what others are doing, but the end result will not always be the same. It is better to brainstorm with your team to come up with something that will help your organization in particular stand out.

Take the vision and mission of your organization seriously— because they will shape everything to follow.

CHAPTER FOUR

DIVISION OF LABOR

One of the most challenging parts of leadership is dealing with different departments in an organization. One important key to handling different departments is having an effective structure in place. Organizational structure arranges the different departments of an organization in a way that maximizes productivity and enables goals to be efficiently accomplished. Structure includes policy manuals that explain the expectations for each aspect of the organization. An effective structure helps everyone avoid confusion, and it maintains order and unity.[15]

This is as true for churches as it is for other types of organizations. The concept of the division of labor in church leadership is rooted in the Bible. The Bible tells us about different roles, or offices, that have different functions but work towards the same vision of the church:

> So Christ himself gave the apostles, the prophets, the evangelists, the pastors and teachers, **12** to equip his people for works of service, so that the body of Christ may be built up. — Ephesians 4:11–12 (NIV)

Therefore, the five offices are prophet, pastor, teacher, apostle, and evangelist—also called the five-fold ministries. They are not a system of rank, but rather the main departments in the church. Within each one there are other spiritual gifts operating. Let's take a look at the basic job descriptions for these offices.

The Prophet

The book *Prophecy: Understanding and Utilizing the Manifestation of Prophecy* describes the role of the prophet this way:

> First and foremost, the prophet is a "spokesman" for God. The prophet must be able to hear the voice of God and bring God's words to the world.[16]

Prophets do the following things:[17]

- **"Tell what will happen in the future."** (1 Samuel 10:1–6; Isaiah 52:13–53:12; Acts 11:28, 21:11)
- **"Speak of past events."** (Judges 6:7–10; 2 Samuel 12:7–8; Ezekiel 20:1–31; John 4:18)

- **"Strengthen"**; that is, "edification" (KJV). (2 Samuel 7:8–12; Haggai 2:1–5)
- **"Exhort."** (2 Chronicles 15:1–7; Isaiah 35:1–4; Haggai 1:3–12)
- **"Comfort."** (2 Chronicles 20:15–17; Jeremiah 45:1–5)
- **"Bless."** (Deuteronomy 33:1)
- **"Curse."** (2 Kings 2:24; Jeremiah 48:10)
- **"Reprove** (sometimes harshly)." (2 Samuel 12:1–14; Isaiah 22:15–25; Jeremiah 36:30–31; Malachi 2:3; Matthew 16:23, 23:12–36)
- **"Foretell death or disaster."** (1 Samuel 2:27–36; 1 Kings 13:20–24, 22:17–37; Jeremiah 28:16, 29:21; Amos 7:14–17)
- **"Direct."** (Judges 4:4–6; 2 Kings 4:1–7, 5:10, 6:8–10; Jeremiah 32:13–15)
- **"Reveal character and what is in a person's heart."** (Isaiah 9:9, 9:17, 29:13, 48:4; Jeremiah 2:21, 5:23; Ezekiel 14:2–4; John 1:47)
- **"Interpret enigmas."** (Daniel 5:5–29)
- **"Reveal what is going on from a spiritual perspective."** (1 Chronicles 5:20; Jeremiah 1:16; Ezekiel 5:11; Daniel 9:11; John 8:42–47)

The Pastor-Teacher

In Ephesians 4:11, the Bible mentions pastors and teachers separately. Christ intended the apostles, the prophets, the evangelists, the pastors, and the teachers "to equip his people for works of service, so that the body of Christ may be built up..."

(Ephesians 4:12 NIV). In practice they function together for the edification of God's people and the furthering of His work. Combining the role of pastor and teacher emphasizes two complementary dimensions of leadership:

1. The term 'pastor' means "shepherd" and emphasizes that the overall function of a pastor is to oversee and lead a flock.
2. The term 'teacher' emphasizes [their] responsibility to provide spiritual nourishment to the sheep that God has allotted to [them].[18]

In Romans 12 there are six active gifts a pastor-teacher can perform in a church: ministry, teaching, exhortation, giving, ruling, and mercy.[19] Some of the qualifying characteristics to carry out these functions as a pastor-teacher include:

- a student of Biblical doctrine (1 Timothy 4:6, 4:11, 4:13; 2 Timothy 2:15)

- able and prepared to teach (1 Timothy 3:2; 2 Timothy 2:2, 24, 4:2)

- able to reprove severely with sound teaching rebellious men and deceivers (Titus 1:10-13)

- an administrator (Titus 1:7; 1 Timothy 3:4)

- a servant of the Lord (2 Timothy 2:24)

- self-disciplined (1 Timothy 3:2, 4:7, 4:8; Titus 1:8)

- faithful and consistent (2 Timothy 2:2, 3:14, 3:15; 1 Timothy 1:12; Ephesians 6:21; Colossians 1:7; Colossians 4:7)
- above reproach (Titus 1:6; 1 Timothy 3:2)
- a good example (1 Timothy 4:12; 1 Peter 5:2, 5:3)
- maintaining a good reputation with unbelievers (1 Timothy 3:7; 2 Corinthians 8:21)
- care for the congregation (1 Timothy 3:5)
- mature, not a new convert (1 Timothy 3:6)
- able to handle rejection. (1 Thessalonians 2:2, 4:1–8; Colossians 1:24)
- a devoted spouse and effective parent (Titus 1:6; 1 Timothy 3:2, 3:4)
- gentle (1 Timothy 3:3; 2 Timothy 2:25)
- patient (2 Timothy 2:24, 4:2)
- hospitable (1 Timothy 3:2; Titus 1:8)
- not arrogant or quick-tempered (Titus 1:7)
- uncontentious (1 Timothy 3:3; 2 Timothy 2:24)
- not be a gossip (1 Timothy 3:11)
- not be a lover of money (1 Timothy 3:3; Titus 1:7)
- sensible, just, and devout (Titus 1:8)

- not an alcoholic (1 Timothy 3:2–3; Titus 1:7)

If God truly has called you to be a shepherd, He will take good care of you. However, if you jump into it because you want to be like others, you will hurt the sheep and yourself. It is a higher calling with great demand and a lot of responsibility.

The Apostle[20]

In essence, an apostle is someone sent to represent the person who sends him. An apostle will often bring a message from the one who sent them, or will work to accomplish the purposes of the sender. If a church sends an apostle, the latter is sent to represent the church and its mission.

The great commission gives a description of what apostles are called to do:

> Go ye therefore, and teach all nations, baptizing them in the name of the Father, and of the Son, and of the Holy Ghost: Teaching them to observe all things whatsoever I have commanded you: and, lo, I am with you always, even unto the end of the world. — Matthew 28:19–20 (KJV)

> ... you shall be witnesses to Me in Jerusalem, and in all Judea and Samaria, and to the end of the earth. — Acts 1:8 (NKJV)

In the beginning of the church, they did not have the complete Scriptures we have today. The apostles of Christ were the main, and only, source for direction from God:

> But *Peter, standing up with the eleven,* raised his voice and said to them ... "Repent, and let every one of you be baptized in the name of Jesus Christ for the remission of sins; and you shall receive the gift of the Holy Spirit. For the promise is to you and to your children, and to all who are afar off, as many as the Lord our God will call." And with many other words he testified and exhorted them, saying, "Be saved from this perverse generation." Then those who gladly received his word were baptized; and that day about three thousand souls were added to them. And they *continued steadfastly in the apostles' doctrine and fellowship,* in the breaking of bread, and in prayers. Then fear came upon every soul, and *many wonders and signs were done through the apostles.* — Acts 2:14, 2:38–43 (NKJV)

Apostles spoke the words of God, and He allowed signs and wonders to follow them so people could see they were truly sent by Him. Jesus told His apostles:

> These things I have spoken to you while being present with you. But the Helper, *the Holy Spirit,*

whom the Father will send in My name, He will *teach you all things,* and *bring to your remembrance all things* that I said to you. — John 14:25–26 (NKJV)

However, when He, the Spirit of truth, has come, He will guide you into *all truth*; for He will not speak on His own authority, but whatever He hears He will speak; and He will tell you things to come. — John 16:13 (NKJV)

The apostles were chosen by Jesus and they spoke His words. They truly represented Him in the world. They carried His authority and fulfilled His will. They were also eyewitnesses of His ministry and of His resurrection.

In the New Testament the apostles: planted churches (1 Corinthians 3:10–11, Galatians 1:6-10, 3:1); took the gospel to unreached places (Romans 15:20); appointed and trained leaders (Acts 14:21–23 and Titus 1:5); dealt with false doctrines and sin (1 Corinthians 1:1–16:24; Acts 15); connected churches and fostered unity (1 Corinthians 16:1–4, Ephesians 4:1–16, Romans 15:25–27); demonstrated and imparted supernatural gifts 2 Timothy 1:6–7, 2 Corinthians 12:12, Acts 4:33, Acts 8:4–20, Acts 10:44–46, Acts 19:16); showed humility in the midst of adversity (1 Corinthians 4:9–13); and were faithful financial stewards (Acts 4:33–37). In addition they would not: manipulate or self-promote (2 Corinthians 11:7–15); demand financial guarantees ((2 Corinthians

12:14–18); or make merchandise of the gospel (John 2:13–17, Hebrews 3:1).[21]

Apostles are commonly associated with missionaries who go to new places and plant a church. Those who spearhead into new places will sometimes have to utilize the other five-fold ministry offices because they are breaking new ground. For example, Paul can be seen in the roles of evangelist, pastor, and teacher. An apostle should also follow up with church plants to ensure they continue to grow.[22]

Moreover, apostles have the opportunity to encourage and minister to those leaders functioning in other offices. Pastors can seek edification and prayer from apostles. Oftentimes pastors become burnt out because they don't have apostles to support them in their ministry. This is the example given in the book of Acts 6:2–3 when a decision for the position of deacon needed to be made.[23]

The five-fold ministries are an essential part of enabling a church to function the way God intended. As a leader of a church or other organization, it is important to seek out those who have different spiritual gifts so that you will not be lacking in any area. Seek out apostles to strengthen your ministry. However, use wisdom in choosing who will fill these roles, as the Bible warns about false apostles:

> For such are false apostles, deceitful workers, transforming themselves into the apostles of Christ? — 2 Corinthians 11:13 (KJV)[24]

You may be able to identify a false prophet if they seem motivated by selfish gain. For this reason, seek out those who will serve selflessly. It is also important that you have a trusting relationship established with them. A true apostle will seek what he can give, not what he will receive.[25]

The Evangelist[26]

What is an evangelist? Easton's Bible Dictionary defines it as a "publisher of glad tidings;" a missionary preacher of the gospel (Ephesians 4:11).[27] In Act 21:8, Philip is called an evangelist. The role of evangelist primarily focuses on preaching the gospel. It can be inferred based on Scripture that an evangelist is distinct from the other five-fold ministries. Smith's Bible Dictionary defines evangelist this way: "The work of the evangelist is the proclamation of the glad tidings to those who have not known them, rather than the instruction and pastoral care of those who have believed and been baptized."[28]

You can therefore conclude that an evangelist is someone who preaches the gospel publicly to those who do not yet believe. An evangelist can benefit the church; however, they primarily work with those who are not yet Christians. In Acts 16:17, a slave-girl in Philippi said, "These men are servants of the Most High God, who proclaim to us the way of salvation" (NKJV).

We know from Romans 10 that people must be given the opportunity to be saved by hearing the message. It says:

> But how are men to call upon him in whom they have not believed? And how are they to believe in him of whom they have never heard? And how are they to hear without a preacher?" — Romans 10:14 (RSV)

This is the most important role of the evangelist—to give people the opportunity to hear and believe.

In preaching and teaching to people within and outside of the church, evangelists act as spiritual soldiers in God's army, and as stewards or caretakers of His Word.

The specific functions of the offices and other spiritual gifts described in the Bible will vary from one church or ministry to another, as specific leadership duties will vary from any type of organization to another.

Additionally, even if all of the departments start to function properly, the work is not finished—the leaders of those departments need frequent training. You also have to make sure regularly that they are all following the church or organizational vision and cooperating in pursuit of the mission.

Some people can discover their gift at an early stage of their spiritual journey, while others need help in order for them to know what their gift is. It is the responsibility of an organization's leader to help department leaders and other members to understand their gifts and their roles, and to coordinate their efforts effectively and respectfully. All departments are needed in some form.

Remember, anybody can start a church or an organization, but not everybody can grow it. It takes a qualified team and the whole membership working together for an organization to become spiritually healthy and effective in its God-intended purpose.

CHAPTER FIVE

THE CHARACTER OF A LEADER

Character is the substance of how we live our lives. It is something that can be taught—but ultimately an individual must make a choice for themselves about what kind of person they are going to be. You must choose for yourself to live a life of character, as numerous men and women in the Bible did:

> Several people in the Bible are described as having noble character: Ruth (Ruth 3:11), Hanani (Nehemiah 7:2), David (Psalm 78:72), and Job (Job 2:3). These individuals' lives were distinguished by persistent moral virtue. Character is influenced and developed by our choices... We can develop character by controlling our thoughts

(Philippians 4:8), practicing Christian virtues (2 Peter 1:5–6), guarding our hearts (Proverbs 4:23; Matthew 15:18-20), and keeping good company (1 Corinthians 15:33).[29]

God created us in His image, and this includes His character. We can blame society for our inability to practice what is right. However, if a leader wants to change and transform others, their own character must be a top priority. Your character is important because it defines who you are as a leader. Here are some of the characteristics that will help you effectively lead the people God has entrusted to you.

A Character of Discipline

> Whoever loves discipline loves knowledge, but whoever hates correction is stupid. — Proverbs 12:1 (NIV)

Discipline keeps you accountable to instruction from God and those who have an influence in your life. It is an essential part of learning and growing in your role as a leader.[30] Discipline can protect you from being misdirected in your leadership. Allowing yourself to be open to discipline will help you be the best leader you can be.

A leader can both discipline and be disciplined. The rules and regulations in an organization should be applied to everybody. The Bible says in Hebrews 12:11, "No discipline seems pleasant at the time, but painful. Later on, however, it produces a harvest of righteousness and peace for those who have been trained by it" (NIV). Avoiding discipline can lead to a lack of order in your ministry and hinder the fulfillment of your vision.

A Character of Integrity

> The integrity of the upright guides them, but the unfaithful are destroyed by their duplicity. — Proverbs 11:3 (NIV)

Integrity is a crucial character trait for a leader. A person of integrity acts with honesty, fairness, and sincerity. A leader who is faithful to keep their word has integrity.[31] Walking with integrity is a challenge for a lot of leaders. Many leaders are struggling to lead with integrity because of their desire for material gain. The Bible says in Proverbs 28:6, however, "Better is a poor man who walks in his integrity than a rich man who is crooked in his ways" (ESV). There is a reward for leading with integrity instead of dishonesty, and "whoever walks in integrity walks securely, but he who makes his ways crooked will be found out" (Proverbs 10:9 ESV).

A Character of Obedience

> But Samuel replied: "Does the LORD delight in burnt offerings and sacrifices as much as in obeying the LORD? To obey is better than sacrifice,

and to heed is better than the fat of rams." — 1 Samuel 15:22 (NIV)

Leaders can easily be swept away by fame and can even begin to think and act as if they are God. Obedience keeps us in alignment with what God has commanded in His word. It ensures that we stay close to Him in every circumstance.[32] The Bible says in Romans 5:19, "For just as through the disobedience of the one man the many were made sinners, so also through the obedience of the one man the many will be made righteous" (NIV). Therefore, if a leader is obedient to God, this will have a positive impact on their followers. In contrast, disobedience will have a negative impact on them. God rejected Saul as a king because of disobedience:

> For rebellion is as the sin of witchcraft, and stubbornness is as iniquity and idolatry. Because thou hast rejected the word of the LORD, he hath also rejected thee from being king. — 1 Samuel 15:23 (KJV)

Disobedience, then, is comparable to witchcraft, which is very serious. If you walk in obedience, meanwhile, it will be a blessing to you and you followers.

A Character of Gratitude

> We ought always to thank God for you, brothers and sisters, and rightly so, because your faith is

> growing more and more, and the love all of you have for one another is increasing. — 2 Thessalonians 1:3 (NIV)

An effective leader lives a life of thankfulness and regularly expresses their appreciation to God and others.[33] The Bible says, "In everything give thanks; for this is the will of God in Christ Jesus for you" (1 Thessalonians 5:18 NKJV). Expressing thankfulness is a dimension of worship. It recognizes the good things God has done for you and also places value on the people in your life.[34][35] A leader who knows how to show gratitude to God and the people around them will never run out of ideas. Jesus told His disciples this story in Luke 17:11–17:

> On his way to Jerusalem, Jesus went along the border between Samaria and Galilee. **12** As he was going into a village, ten men with leprosy came toward him. They stood at a distance **13** and shouted, "Jesus, Master, have pity on us!" **14** Jesus looked at them and said, "Go show yourselves to the priests." On their way they were healed. **15** When one of them discovered that he was healed, he came back, shouting praises to God. **16** He bowed down at the feet of Jesus and thanked him. The man was from the country of Samaria. **17** Jesus asked, "Weren't ten men healed? Where are the other nine? (CEV)

Unlike the tenth leper, when things are going well, we may forget where we started and the people who were with us during difficult times. The Israelites forgot God: "You turned away from

God, your Creator; you forgot the Mighty Rock, the source of your life" (Deuteronomy 32:18 CEV). If you humble yourself and let others know how much you appreciate their contribution to your life, you will never lack their support.

A Teachable Character

> Instruct the wise and they will be wiser still; teach the righteous and they will add to their learning
> — Proverbs 9:9 (NIV)

Being teachable means being willing to learn. A teachable person accepts correction and learns from every situation in life. They don't think they know more than everybody: "Whoever loves discipline loves knowledge, but whoever hates correction is stupid" (Proverbs 12:1 NIV). In every season of life, you can learn from anyone and anything. Here are things you can observe from someone with a teachable character:[36][37]

- You know that you have limitations.
- You allow others to know about your areas of weakness.
- You are willing to let others help and guide you.
- You seek to learn from everyone around you.
- You are willing to take a risk even if it means initial failure.
- If you do fail, you receive help and continue to work towards success.
- You invite counsel into your life.

- You seek to learn each and every day.
- You believe everyone has something to teach you.
- You know that there is a benefit to each new thing you learn.

A Discerning Character[38]

> And it is my prayer that your love may abound more and more, with knowledge and all discernment, so that you may approve what is excellent, and so be pure and blameless for the day of Christ. — Philippians 1:9–10 (ESV)

Discernment uses wisdom to determine what is just, fair, and right in any given circumstance. Walking in discernment allows you to put aside your own opinions and make choices based in the truth. It is important for a leader to settle a dispute without been biased. The Bible says in John 7:24, "Do not judge by appearances, but judge with right judgment" (ESV). This character trait leads you to take the time to look into circumstances before coming to a conclusion in a matter. A leader with discernment does not make decisions rashly.

A Character of Tolerance

> With all lowliness and meekness, with longsuffering, forbearing one another in love… — Ephesians 4:2 (KJV)

Tolerance recognizes that everyone is at a different place spiritually and that we all serve a different function in the body of Christ. A leader who possesses tolerance will be patient with those who are weaker and will seek to understand those who are different from them. A tolerant leader endeavors to keep others from evil, while also avoiding being judgmental.[39]

The book of Romans 14:1–4 says:

> As for the one who is weak in faith, welcome him, but not to quarrel over opinions. One person believes he may eat anything, while the weak person eats only vegetables. Let not the one who eats despise the one who abstains, and let not the one who abstains pass judgment on the one who eats, for God has welcomed him. Who are you to pass judgment on the servant of another? It is before his own master that he stands or falls. And he will be upheld, for the Lord is able to make him stand. (ESV)

A Character of Humility

> For everyone who exalts himself will be humbled, and he who humbles himself will be exalted — Luke 14:11 (ESV)

> ...not lording it over those entrusted to you, but being examples to the flock. 4 And when the Chief Shepherd appears, you will receive the crown of glory that will never fade away. 5 In the same way, you who are younger, submit

> yourselves to your elders. All of you, clothe yourselves with humility toward one another, because, "God opposes the proud but shows favor to the humble." — 1 Peter 5:3–5 (NIV)

Humility means walking without pride. A humble person recognizes that it is a weakness to think they are better than others. It helps you remember that you are not superior to others just because you are a leader. A humble leader does not consider anyone unworthy of their time and attention.[40]

To be a leader doesn't make you better than those you are taking care of. Remember that you need the help of those around you—you can't work alone. The apostle Paul said, in Romans 12:3:

> For by the grace given to me I say to everyone among you not to think of himself more highly than he ought to think, but to think with sober judgment, each according to the measure of faith that God has assigned. (ESV)

A Character of Fairness

> Open your mouth, judge righteously, defend the rights of the poor and needy. — Proverbs 31:9 (ESV)

Fairness gives equal opportunity to all parties involved in a situation. A fair leader makes decisions with equity. Leading with fairness means giving up the right to put ourselves or anyone else unjustly before another. Being fair means leading without prejudice or partiality.[41]

A Character of Friendship[42]

> I no longer call you servants, because a servant does not know his master's business. Instead, I have called you friends, for everything that I learned from my Father I have made known to you. — John 15:15 (NIV)

Being friendly as a leader is very important. Jesus treated His disciples as friends—a good example for every leader to emulate. It will help those you are working with to be open about their struggles and challenges. Friendship connects us to one another and allows us to play an integral role in each other's lives. Friends help each other become the people God wants them to be. A friend is also willing to share what God has blessed them with.

A Character of Efficiency

> Whoever can be trusted with very little can also be trusted with much, and whoever is dishonest with very little will also be dishonest with much. — Luke 16:10 (NIV)

Efficiency means doing whatever it takes to get things done in an orderly and timely fashion. An efficient leader is not lazy, but rather seeks the best course of action for achieving their goals.

Being efficient is made possible by being organized and making the most of your time. Seeking the best way to do things will allow you to achieve the greatest effectiveness.[43]

There is a reward for those who are well organized. As it is written in Matthew 25:21, "Well-done, good and faithful servant! You have been faithful with a few things; I will put you in charge of many things. Come and share your master's happiness!" (NIV).

A Character of Encouragement

> Therefore encourage one another and build each other up, just as in fact you are doing — 1 Thessalonians 5:11 (NIV)

Encouragement lifts up those who are downtrodden in life by speaking God's truth into their situation.[44] We need encouragement every day of our lives. The book of Hebrews 10:24–25 says, "And let us consider how to stir up one another to love and good works, not neglecting to meet together, as is the habit of some, but encouraging one another, and all the more as you see the Day drawing near" (ESV).

A Character of Punctuality

> Walk in wisdom toward outsiders, making the best use of the time. — Colossians 4:5 (ESV)

Punctuality is important because it communicates that you value people's time. We are commissioned to make the most of the time we are given, and punctuality is an expression of that principle. When you are punctual, it communicates to others that you care about and respect them.[45]

In short, a leader must take time seriously:

> Look carefully then how you walk, not as unwise but as wise, making the best use of the time, because the days are evil. — Ephesians 5:15–16 (ESV)

A Character of Attentiveness

> My dear brothers and sisters, take note of this: Everyone should be quick to listen, slow to speak and slow to become angry. — James 1:19 (NIV)

Attentiveness also expresses value to others because it shows that you care about what they communicate with their words and their lives. It is another way to put the needs of others above your own.[46]

Sometimes it is good to be silent as a leader and listen to what others have to say. We can learn and benefit from listening to others:

> He who restrains his words has knowledge, and he who has a cool spirit is a man of understanding. — Proverbs 17:27 (NASB)

If we are quick to speak and not listen, the Bible says in the Proverbs 29:20, "Do you see a man who is hasty in his words? There is more hope for a fool than for him" (NASB).

A Character of Compassion

> So, as those who have been chosen of God, holy and beloved, put on a heart of compassion, kindness, humility, gentleness and patience... — Colossians 3:12 (NASB)

Compassion takes into consideration what other people are going through. A compassionate person stands with others and helps them carry their burdens. A leader with compassion will enter into the pain and suffering of those in their care. This kind of compassion is a deep expression of love.[47]

The Bible commands us, "Be kind and compassionate to one another, forgiving each other, just as in Christ God forgave you" (Ephesians 4:32 NIV).

A leader can be firm while also being compassionate. When Jesus heard that Lazarus was dead, He cried (John 11:35). Always put yourself into the shoes of others and see how it feels, "To sum up, all of you be harmonious, sympathetic, brotherly, kindhearted, and humble in spirit... (1 Peter 3:8 NASB).

A Character of Flexibility

> I can do all things through him who strengthens me. — Philippians 4:13 (ESV)

It is easy for a leader to become rigid and unapproachable. Sometimes people are afraid to suggest an idea because their leader is resistant to change. A flexible person makes space for new ideas from others, and gives room for positive change. Remaining flexible is essential for establishing healthy relationships that bend to meet current needs.[48]

Some things may not sound right to you initially—but if you are flexible and allow change to happen, it will make sense when the benefits have been reaped. For example, God said this to Abraham when He told him to leave his country:

> Now the LORD had said unto Abram, Get thee out of thy country, and from thy kindred, and from thy father's house, unto a land that I will shew thee... — Genesis 12:1 (KJV)

A Character of Boldness

> Be strong and courageous, because you will lead these people to inherit the land I swore to their ancestors to give them. 7 Be strong and very courageous. Be careful to obey all the law my servant Moses gave you; do not turn from it to the right or to the left, that you may be successful wherever you go... 9 Have I not commanded you? Be strong and courageous. Do not be afraid; do not be discouraged, for the Lord your God will be with you wherever you go. — Joshua 1:6–9 (NIV)

"Be strong and courageous" is repeated three times in this passage, and it came directly from God to Joshua. God knew Joshua would face different challenges, so He encouraged him to be bold and stand for what is right. Being bold means being willing to do what is right no matter what the cost may be. Doing the right thing will not always be easy, and it may be risky and scary at times. However, a bold leader will be able to speak the truth without fear because they know it is the honorable thing to do. Boldness is an expression of trust that God will care for those who are obedient to His precepts.[49]

In contrast to a bold leader, Aaron was a coward in his leadership, and because of that he listened to his followers and made an idol for them:

> Do not be angry, my lord," Aaron answered. "You know how prone these people are to evil. **23** They said to me, 'Make us gods who will go before us. As for this fellow Moses who brought us up out of Egypt, we don't know what has happened to him.' **24** So I told them, 'Whoever has any gold jewelry, take it off.' Then they gave me the gold, and I threw it into the fire, and out came this calf!" **25** Moses saw that the people were running wild and that Aaron had let them get out of control and so become a laughingstock to their enemies. — Exodus 32:22–25 (NIV)

If a leader is not bold, people will disrespect them and they will follow the people. A leader has to be bold in order to stand firm.

The book of Galatians 5:22–23 lists the fruit of the Holy Spirit:[50]

> **Love** will enable us to appreciate our brothers and sisters in the Lord, and, of course, our family, and others around us. Love is taking the initiative to build up and meet the needs of others without expecting anything in return.
>
> **Joy** will allow us to enjoy His creation, others, and our circumstances with an expression of delight and real, authentic happiness from and with harmony with God and others
>
> **Peace** is surrendering and yielding to the Lord's control, for He is our ultimate peace! It is allowing tranquility to be our tone and to control our equanimity. This will be fueled by our harmonious relationship with God so we can hand over control of our heart, will, and mind to Him. Once we make real peace with God, we will be able to make and maintain peace with others.
>
> **Patience** is showing tolerance and fortitude to others, and even accepting difficult situations from them and God without making demands and conditions.
>
> **Kindness** is practicing benevolence and a loving attitude towards others.

Goodness displays integrity, honesty, and compassion to others, and allows us to do the right thing.

Faithfulness is the "gluing" fruit that will preserve our faith and the other characters of the Spirit as well as identify God's Will so we can be dependable and trusting to God and others.

Gentleness is the character that will show calmness, personal care, and tenderness in meeting the needs of others.

Self-Control will allow us to have discipline, and restraint with obedience to God and others.

Therefore, above all, an effective leader of good character must habitually be loving, joyful, peaceful, patient, kind, good, faithful, gentle, and self-controlled.

CHAPTER SIX

GROWING YOUR LEADERSHIP SKILLS

Leadership is like a living organism—you have to grow in order to reproduce your kind. Growth is essential for every leader irrespective of your level of experience. One thing about growth is it does not come quickly or easily. Before a leader can grow, there are many things that need to be considered.

After the death of Moses, God told Joshua to take over Moses' leadership position. God gave specific instructions to Joshua. God told him that if he wanted to be successful and profitable, he had to take certain things seriously. Here is what God said to Joshua:

> No one will be able to stand against you all the days of your life. As I was with Moses, so I will be

> with you; I will never leave you nor forsake you. **6** Be strong and courageous, because you will lead these people to inherit the land I swore to their ancestors to give them. **7** *"Be strong and very courageous. Be careful to obey all the law my* servant Moses gave you; do not turn from it to the right or to the left, that you may be successful wherever you go. **8** *Keep this Book of the Law always on your lips; meditate on it day and night, so that you may be careful to do everything written in it.* Then you will be prosperous and successful. **9** Have I not commanded you? Be strong and courageous. Do not be afraid; do not be discouraged, for the Lord your God will be with you wherever you go.
> — Joshua 1:5–9 (NIV)

God knew that Joshua would face opposition and personal challenges, but encouraged him to be courageous and stand firm. It is not easy to lead people if you don't prepare yourself well. He added that Joshua should keep the Law of Moses— which is the Word of God—and meditate on it day and night. God told him that if he carefully did all the things written, he would prosper and be successful. God promised Joshua that He would never leave him nor forsake him. Joshua might have been younger than the people God told him to lead. However, despite his inexperience, Joshua was able to lead the Israelites to the Promised Land because he obeyed the instruction of God.

Therefore, we too need to feed on the Word of God to be healthy Christians (Jeremiah 15:16; John 6). We do this through the following actions or habits:[51]

- We need to **hear** the Word of God (Nehemiah 9:3).
- We need to **search the Word** after hearing, by reading it (Acts 17:11) (1 Timothy 4:13).
- We need to **study** the Word for understanding (2 Timothy 2:15; 1 Corinthians 10:32–33).
- We need to **memorize** the Word of God so that it dwells with us always (Proverbs 6:21–22).
- We need to **meditate** on the Word of God so that it can nourish us (Joshua 1:3, 1:8).
- We need to **apply** the Word of God so that it becomes the substance of our lives (James 1:22–24).

The Word of God

Joshua 1:5–9 makes clear what God thinks and desires of us. It reveals all He has done and all He will do—and lets us know that those who seek to understand God's Word will find direction and nourishment in the Scriptures. Christians should fill themselves to overflowing with the Word of God! As we read: "All Scripture is breathed out by God and profitable for teaching, for reproof, for correction, and for training in righteousness…" (2 Timothy 3:16 NIV).[52]

After all, every living organism has to eat in order to survive and grow, and the Word of God is food for our spirit. The following scriptures testify to this:

> Then he said to me, "Son of man, eat this scroll I am giving you and fill your stomach with it." So I ate it, and it tasted as sweet as honey in my mouth." — Ezekiel 3:3 (NIV)
>
> How sweet are your words to my taste, sweeter than honey to my mouth. — Psalm 119:103 (NIV)
>
> When your words came, I ate them; they were my joy and my heart's delight, for I bear your name, LORD God Almighty. — Jeremiah 15:16 (NIV)
>
> But you, son of man, listen to what I say to you. Do not rebel like that rebellious people; open your mouth and eat what I give you. — Ezekiel 2:8 (NIV)
>
> I have not departed from the command of his lips; I have treasured the words of his mouth more than my daily bread. — Job 23:12 (NIV)

How do we eat the Word of God? We eat the Word of God by meditating on it day and night. 'Meditation' is "intentional contemplation on the author's work with the express purpose of reflecting upon it, contemplative thinking, the revolving of a subject in the mind or a self-directed practice of calming the mind and body." [53] When a Christian meditates, they are setting their minds to fill themselves up with God's Word.

If reading the Word is like eating, then meditating on the Word is like regurgitation. Something regurgitated has typically been taken in, at least partially digested, and then spit out. This can be done literally (in the physical), or figuratively (in the mental). The Merriam-Webster dictionary says:

> The word often appears in biological contexts (e.g., in describing how some birds feed their chicks by regurgitating incompletely digested food), or in references to ideas or information that have been acquired and restated. A student, for example, might be expected to learn information from a textbook or a teacher and then regurgitate it for a test.[54]

To regurgitate the Word of God—which is food for our spirit—we need to read it and take some time to ponder it deeply. It means, thinking about what you read and then practicing what you read. After reading, you should ask questions if you don't understand. Cultivate a habit of reading the Bible every day. Don't merely read the Bible to dispute facts and debate with others.. You take care of your body by eating three meals a day, you should do the same thing for your spirit by reading the Word of God daily.

Benefits of Meditating on the Word[55]

Meditating on the Word of God has numerous benefits for every believer, but is even more important for leaders.

> Oh how I love your law! It is my meditation all the day. — Psalm 119:97 (ESV)

Meditating on God's Word will lead to an even deeper love for His law because it will enable you to understand the meaning behind the law. As you meditate on His Word, you will understand that it is given to help you and protect you—and those you lead—from harm.

> May my meditation be pleasing to him, for I rejoice in the LORD. — Psalm 104:34 (ESV)

When you meditate on God's Word, it is pleasing to Him, and meditating on the Word can bring you pure joy in turn! There is a lot going on in this world, and most of the things we see and hear every day are negative and discouraging. Yet the Word of God gives us hope and motivation for our spiritual and physical journey.

> I will meditate on your precepts and fix my eyes on your ways. — Psalm 119:15 (ESV)

Fixing your eyes on God's ways can mean giving your full attention to a specific aspect of God's Word. You can pick a verse that carries truth and meaning to your heart and focus on it throughout the day. The more you think on it, the more God can speak to you through it.

> My mouth shall speak wisdom; the meditation of my heart shall be understanding. — Psalm 49:3 (ESV)

Meditating on God's Word brings understanding, and that enables you to speak His wisdom. So fill yourself to overflowing with His understanding and wisdom!

> Even though princes sit plotting against me, your servant will meditate on your statutes. — Psalm 119:24 (ESV)

You can also have peace in the middle of difficult times when you meditate on God's Word. The Word will reassure you of His promises and fill you with a great trust. The more you meditate on God's Word, the less you will be filled with worry.

The Bible remains the only source of divine revelation that can sustain you as a leader. If you meditate on the Word of God daily, it will help you grow in these ways:

- **Truth:** "Sanctify them by Your truth; Your word is truth" (John 17:17 NKJV).[56]

- **God's blessing:** "But He said, 'More than that, blessed are those who hear the word of God and keep it!'" (Luke 11:28 NKJV).[57]
- **Victory:** "...the sword of the Spirit, which is the word of God..." (Ephesians 6:17 NKJV).[58]
- **Growth:** "...as newborn babes, desire the pure milk of the word, that you may grow thereby" (1 Peter 2:2 NKJV).[59]
- **Power:** "For I am not ashamed of the gospel of Christ, for it is the power of God to salvation for everyone who believes, for the Jew first and also for the Greek" (Romans 1:16 NKJV).[60]
- **Guidance:** "Your word is a lamp to my feet and a light to my path" (Psalms 119:105 NKJV).[61]
- **Comfort in affliction:** "The Word of God is our comfort in affliction. (Psalm 19:49–50) Jesus told his disciples, 'In this world you will have tribulation' (John 16:33 NKJV)."[62]
- **Fight off temptation:** "The Word of God is also a weapon to be used to fight off temptation. While in the wilderness, Jesus responded to every instance of temptation by saying, 'It is written...' or 'It is said...' (Luke 4:1–12). Studying the Word of God helps us fight off temptation just as Jesus did."[63]
- **Our thoughts and ideas:** "Studying the Word of God also helps us keep our thoughts and ideas in line with God. Apostle Paul states imaginations and every high thing that exalts itself against the knowledge of God should be cast down. (2 Corinthians 10:5–6) This

includes our own thoughts (Isaiah 55:6–9) as well as heresies that plague the Body of Christ. (Galatians 2:11; Titus 1:11–12)"[64]

Choose a verse from the Bible and meditate on it day and night. This will lead to success (Joshua 1:8)! You can claim this as a promise from God and trust that He will be faithful to keep His Word.

Prayer

In the same way that the Word of God is food for our spirit, praying is like breathing—live-giving air to our spirit. It should be as natural to pray as it is to breathe. In the Bible, God commands us to pray (Philippians 4:6–7). Prayer is exemplified for us by Christ and the early church (Mark 1:35; Acts 1:14, 2:42, 3:1, 4:23–31, 6:4, 13:1–3). If Jesus thought it was worthwhile to pray, we should also. If He needed to pray to remain in the Father's will, how much more do we need to pray?

Another reason to pray is because it is the means for obtaining God's solutions in a number of situations. We pray in preparation for major decisions (Luke 6:12–13); to overcome demonic barriers (Matthew 17:14–21); to gather workers for the spiritual harvest (Luke 10:2); to gain strength to overcome temptation (Matthew 26:41); and to obtain the means of strengthening others spiritually (Ephesians 6:18-19). For situations in which we do not know God's will specifically, prayer is a means of discerning His will. A lack of prayer demonstrates a lack of faith and trust in God's Word. We pray to demonstrate our faith that God will do as He has promised in His Word and will bless our lives abundantly more than we could ask or hope for (Ephesians 3:20). Prayer is our primary means of seeing God work in the lives of others.

Notable prayers from the Bible include:[65]

- Jesus' high priestly prayer (John 17)
- Daniel's prayer for revival and restoration (Daniel 9)
- Nehemiah's prayer for revival and restoration (Nehemiah 1)
- Ezra's prayer for the people's sins (Ezra 9)
- Prayer of Jabez (1 Chronicles 4:10)
- Solomon's dedication of the temple (2 Chronicles 6) and God's answer (2 Chronicles 7:1–14)
- Hezekiah's prayer for victory (2 Kings 18:13–19:37)
- Jehoshaphat's prayer for victory (2 Chronicles 20)
- Job's turning point Job 42:1–6, and victory (Job 42:10)
- Hannah's prevailing, fasting, weeping surrender to God (1 Samuel 1:1–28)
- Habakkuk's prayer (Habakkuk 2:1, 3:2, 3:17–19)
- Jonah's prayer of repentance (Jonah 2)
- The Lord's Prayer (Matthew 6:9–13, Luke 11:2–4)
- Elijah's prayer (1 Kings 17, James 5:17)
- Peter's prayer for raising Dorcas from the dead (Acts 9:40)
- Elisha's prayer for sight and blindness (2 Kings 6:17–18)

- Elijah's prayer for raising the widow's son from the dead (1 Kings 17:20–22)

A leader who wants to grow—and stay spiritually, physically, and emotionally strong—must live a life in prayer. It is a way to communicate with God for direction when making decisions great and small. If you regularly draw closer to God through prayer and reading His Word, you will receive a great message from God on how to lead your followers.

More Ways to Grow as a Leader

In closing, here are some other practical ways for a leader to grow:[66]

Seek out wise counsel. As a leader, you can benefit from the experience of those who possess wisdom in areas where you may lack it. Seek out these wise counselors and position yourself to learn from them. You will need at least one person to mentor you. You can have mentors who teach you personally, and you can also glean wisdom from reputable books. Don't ever stop learning no matter how smart you think you are. You have to humble yourself before you can acquire knowledge and wisdom.

Receive direction. It can be challenging to have someone else tell us we have done something incorrectly. However, being willing to take direction provides us with the opportunity to change for the better. If you allow others to correct you, you will be posturing yourself for success in the future.

Teach others to lead. If you are teaching other people how to lead, you will be strengthening your own ability to lead as well. Jesus said in Luke 6:38, "when we give, it will be given back to us." The more you teach others, the more you will improve and grow as a leader. Sometimes leaders are afraid that the leaders they train will become a threat to their position. However, a good leader shouldn't be afraid of losing their position in the organization.

Identify strengths and weaknesses. It is important for a leader to recognize their strengths and weaknesses. You should be able to evaluate what areas you are doing well in, and what areas you need to grow in. All of us as human beings have weaknesses, but as a leader, it is dangerous for you them. Are you confident enough to recognize your strengths and weaknesses?

Do not fear failure. Failure is not defeat. If you fail as a leader, it is not the end of your endeavors. Failure is merely the cost of taking risks and pursuing growth. If you do not fear failure, it will help you mature as a leader. Don't let failure become an obstacle for you in your leadership. Always learn from your failure and make the corrections needed so you can try again. Don't be afraid to fall short and try again! Be flexible and open to taking challenging risks. Successful people don't see failure as an enemy, but rather as a stepping-stone to help them climb higher.

Above all, leaders need the desire to grow. Growth will come naturally if it is truly your priority. If you are willing, you can grow to become the effective leader God created you to be!

CHAPTER SEVEN

TEAMWORK

To be a great leader, you must be ready and willing to work with a team. Teamwork offers a lot of benefits to a leader and their organization. When you work with a team, the work-load becomes lighter and everyone can be more efficient. Utilizing a team will enhance your productivity. Teamwork functions best when everyone is seeking to work towards the vision, rather than seeking their own needs.[67]

God was the first to initiate the concept of teamwork during creation, specifically when He created human beings. Then God said, "Let us make mankind in our image, in our likeness, so that they may rule over the fish in the sea and the birds in the sky, over the livestock and all the wild animals, and over all the creatures that move along the ground" (Genesis 1:26 NIV).

God used the phrase "let us," which is an exhortation to the group, inviting them to do something together. The three persons of God worked in unison—as a team, if you will—to create humankind.

When human beings were increasing in numbers, they became increasingly disobedient to God. When God decided to confuse men with many languages, He also did so in the "team" of the Holy Trinity:

> But the LORD came down to see the city and the tower the people were building. **6** The LORD said, "If as one people speaking the same language they have begun to do this, then nothing they plan to do will be impossible for them. **7** Come, let us go down and confuse their language so they will not understand each other. — Genesis 11:5–7 (NIV)

No matter how creative and gifted a leader is, they still need a team to work with. God could have done everything Himself, but He demonstrated teamwork for us to emulate. It is indisputable that working in a team is a challenge, but a leader cannot do everything alone.

Here is the advice Jethro gave to Moses when he saw Moses working alone:

The next morning Moses sat down at the place where he decided legal cases for the people, and everyone crowded around him until evening. **14** Jethro saw how much Moses had to do for the people, and he asked, "Why are you the only judge? Why do you let these people crowd around you from morning till evening?" **15** Moses answered, "Because they come here to find out what God wants them to do. **16** They bring their complaints to me, and I make decisions on the basis of God's laws."

17 Jethro replied:

That isn't the best way to do it. **18** You and the people who come to you will soon be worn out. The job is too much for one person; you can't do it alone. 19 God will help you if you follow my advice. You should be the one to speak to God for the people, **20** and you should teach them God's laws and show them what they must do to live right. **21** You will need to appoint some competent leaders who respect God and are trustworthy and honest. Then put them over groups of ten, fifty, a hundred, and a thousand. **22** These judges can handle the ordinary cases and bring the more difficult ones to you. Having them to share the load will make your work easier. **23** This is the way God wants it done. You won't be under nearly as much stress, and everyone else will return home feeling satisfied.

24 Moses followed Jethro's advice. **25** He chose some competent leaders from every tribe in Israel and put them over groups of ten, fifty, a hundred, and a thousand. **26** They served as judges, deciding the easy cases themselves, but bringing the more difficult ones to Moses. (Exodus 18:13–26 ESV)

Next we will explore some of the benefits of strong teamwork.

Increased Efficiency

Each of you should use whatever gift you have received to serve others, as faithful stewards of God's grace in its various forms. — 1 Peter 4:10 (NIV)

As we discussed earlier, efficiency means doing whatever it takes to get things done in an orderly and timely fashion. An efficient leader is not lazy, and seeks the best course of action for achieving their goals. Being efficient is made possible by being organized and making the most of your time.[68]

When you work with a team, you work together to achieve your vision. A team helps increase efficiency. When you have a team, there are more minds working together to solve problems and present ideas. A team naturally leads to tasks being accomplished more quickly because the work load is shared by many.[69]

Brainstorming New Ideas

Working with a team provides a leader with many innovative ideas to explore.[70] God wants us to share ideas with each other:

> Then Moses said to the Israelites, "See, the LORD has chosen Bezalel son of Uri, the son of Hur, of the tribe of Judah, **31** and he has filled him with the Spirit of God, with wisdom, with understanding, with knowledge and with all kinds of skills— **32** to make artistic designs for work in gold, silver and bronze, **33** to cut and set stones, to work in wood and to engage in all kinds of artistic crafts. **34** And he has given both him and Oholiab son of Ahisamak, of the tribe of Dan, the ability to teach others. **35** He has filled them with skill to do all kinds of work as engravers, designers, embroiderers in blue, purple and scarlet yarn and fine linen, and weavers—all of them skilled workers and designers. — Exodus 35:30–35 (NIV)

In this passage, God selected Bezalel, who was very gifted and able to do a lot of things. He also chose Oholiab son of Ahisamak, who had the ability to teach others. God knew that if these people came together as a team, they would be able to accomplish His purposes more effectively.

For instance, a team has the benefit of being able to come up with more ideas together than if they worked individually. A leader who fosters an environment that welcomes input encourages everyone to participate in the brainstorming process. Everyone is different, and when we work in a team, we learn from others as part of finding the best solutions.[71]

Learning from Each Other

> Let the wise hear and increase in learning, and the one who understands obtain guidance... — Proverbs 1:5 (ESV)

Indeed, one of the core benefits of working in a team is the opportunity to learn and grow. When a team comes together, they have the ability to speak into each other's lives. They can encourage each other's strengths and help each other in their weaknesses. In a team environment, it is important for everyone to remain teachable. As team members build each other up, everyone will grow in confidence.[72]

Sharing the Workload[73]

> I planted the seed, Apollos watered it, but God has been making it grow. — 1 Corinthians 3:6 (NIV)

A team that works together with the same vision has the opportunity to share the work that needs to be done. The most beneficial way of dividing the work is based on the gifts and strengths of each member. As a team member and leader, you should seek the good of the whole team and serve selflessly.

Having a Support Network[74]

> Two are better than one, because they have a good reward for their toil. For if they fall, one will lift up his fellow. But woe to him who is alone when he falls and has not another to lift him up! **10** Again, if two lie together, they keep warm, but how can one keep warm alone? **11** And though a man might prevail against one who is alone, two will withstand him—a threefold cord is not quickly broken. — Ecclesiastes 4:9–12 (ESV)

The beauty of a team is the amount of encouragement you can bring to each other. As team members, we should seek to build each other up and support each other in work and life. It is important to establish an atmosphere of trust. Therefore, seek each other for guidance and counsel. When challenges arise, we can stand with each other to overcome the situation and walk successfully.

Enhancing Communication

> Iron sharpens iron, and one man sharpens another. — Proverbs 27:17 (ESV)

Teamwork necessarily helps us grow in areas of communication. When we're working with people from different backgrounds, communication is not always easy. We have to learn to communicate effectively with different types of people. Misunderstandings can lead to problems in the organization. It is essential for a team to learn how to understand each other because effective communication helps everyone stay on the same page so that we can better reach our goals.[75]

We need each other to operate as a single organism. We all have weaknesses, but when we work together, we balance each other out. When everyone brings their gifts to the table, we have everything we need. Thus, everyone needs to be involved in ministry for it to be effective. Romans 12 talks about how our bodies won't function properly without each part working together. We need teams, then, in order to be successful.[76]

For example:

> Jesus' twelve-man team was marked by its diversity (Mark 3:13–18; Luke 6:12–16). One was a tax collector,

several were fishermen, one was politically active and known as "the Zealot." The Gospels recount three and a half years of intense training as the disciples spent time at Jesus' side as He taught and ministered to people. At the midpoint of their mentorship, Jesus sent the twelve out in two-man teams (Mark 6:7–13). They were given authority, direction, and opportunity. Jesus followed up with review, correction, and rest (Mark 6:30–31)

Moses, leader of the Israelites and author of the first five books of the Bible, led more than a million people through a nomadic existence that lasted forty years. His earliest teammate was Aaron, his brother (Exodus 6:26–7:20). Later, on the advice of his father-in-law, he added leaders for teams of thousands, hundreds, fifties, and tens (Exodus 24).[77]

However, in order for your team to accomplish their vision, they must have strong teamwork principles capable of overcoming the inevitable moments of conflict.[78]

Conflict Resolution and Cooperation[79]

What causes fights and quarrels among you? Don't they come from your desires that battle within you? — James 4:1 (NIV)

A team working together is bound to come across conflicts eventually, so it is important for a team to work on their conflict resolution skills in order to be effective in accomplishing their goals. Sometimes this will look like putting aside differences and learning to cooperate. In times of conflict, seek out biblical wisdom to find a resolution.

Team Coordination[80]

Coordination is a way of staying organized that will help a team accomplish their goals. A leader must coordinate how the team will work together and how to best allocate their resources. This will enable a team to make deadlines while being as efficient as possible. An example of coordination in the Bible is the account of when Solomon was building a temple for God in Jerusalem:

> King Solomon conscripted laborers from all Israel—thirty thousand men. **14** He sent them off to Lebanon in shifts of ten thousand a month, so that they spent one month in Lebanon and two months at home. Adoniram was in charge of the forced labor. **15** Solomon had seventy thousand carriers and eighty thousand stonecutters in the hills, **16** as well as thirty-three hundred foremen who supervised the project and directed the workers. — 1 Kings 5:13–16 (NIV)

As a result of Solomon's organization in coordinating, they were able to build the Temple on time and according to their specific design. Coordination made their building project successful.

Communicating Clear Expectations[81]

> ...from whom the whole body, joined and held together by every joint with which it is equipped, when each part is working properly, makes the body grow so that it builds itself up in love. — Ephesians 4:16 (ESV)

Communication is essential because it helps everyone stay on the same page with a clear understanding of what needs to be done. A leader needs to communicate to their team what their expectations are.

A team has many different members, as does the body of Christ. Teams will only be successful when everyone is fulfilling the role they are best suited for. When everyone works together, your team will be successful in reaching their goals and, ultimately, in advancing the Kingdom of God.

CHAPTER EIGHT

THE BEST LEADERSHIP MODEL

There are a lot of leadership models available, which makes most leaders wonder which model is the best. The best leadership model will depend on the location, the vision, the mission, and the people involved in the organization. The word 'leader' often connotes someone with power, authority, and control. We assume a leader should be fearless and fearsome. Domineering leaders are sometimes successful; however, their followers may not feel free to be themselves. Instead, they operate in fear and pretend to love what they are doing.

Our Lord Jesus Christ showed us what a true leader should be. The leadership model Jesus demonstrated for us to emulate is called the servant-leadership model.[82] As Paul wrote to the Philippian church:

> Do nothing from rivalry or conceit, but in humility count others more significant than yourselves. **4** Let each of you look not only to his own interests, but also to the interests of others. **5** Have this mind among yourselves, which is yours in Christ Jesus, **6** who, though he was in the form of God, did not count equality with God a thing to be grasped, **7** but made himself nothing, taking the form of a servant, being born in the likeness of men — Philippians 2:3–7 (ESV)

The book of 1 Peter 5:3 says: "…not domineering over those in your charge, but being examples to the flock" (ESV). Jesus demonstrated this kind of leadership to His disciples by washing their feet:

> When he had washed their feet and put on his outer garments and resumed his place, he said to them, "Do you understand what I have done to you? **13** You call me Teacher and Lord, and you are right, for so I am. **14** If I then, your Lord and Teacher, have washed your feet, you also ought to wash one another's feet. **15** For I have given you an example, that you also should do just as I have done to you." — John 13:12–15 (ESV)

Servant-Leadership Explained[83]

> But not so with you. Rather, let the greatest among you become as the youngest, and the leader as one who serves. — Luke 22:26 **(ESV)**

Christian leaders are not supposed to lead in the same way that the world leads. We are not to seek ourselves first, but are to consider the needs of others as greater than our own (Mark 10:42–44; Matthew 20: 25–28). Servant-leadership serves others by investing in their development and well-being. Leadership seeks the good of all and not just personal gain. A servant-leader will empower others to serve God and do His work in the world.

How to Apply Servant-Leadership in an Organization[84]

Servant-leadership in an organization will not put an emphasis on a hierarchical system of rank. Instead, everyone will be an essential part of the team designated to play the role that is best suited for them.

When everyone plays a role that fits with their gifting, there will be an atmosphere of productivity as each person does their part to fulfill the vision. A servant-leader will seek to protect their followers even to their own detriment.

All departments require accountable authorities with the power to make the ministry operational. However, a servant-leader will be open to receiving counsel from others while also taking responsibility for the outcome of any given situation.

Even still, those following a servant-leader should still be held accountable for their actions and be faithful in their responsibilities. At times, the leader may need to bring guidance or correction when necessary. However, this is not to be done lightly and should prioritize the best interest of the one being corrected, and of the group at large.

Leading Through Serving[85]

Servant-leadership is not just reserved for the main overseer of a project—it is for every member in the team. An organization or church that uses a servant-leader model will be most effective when everyone endeavors to serve each other. Every team member participates when there is a struggle, a decision to be made, and the overall outworking of the vision.

Team members should strive for excellence in all they do in order to achieve the highest standards. Servant-leadership within a team looks like each person making an effort to lift each other up in their responsibilities. When everyone balances serving with leading, the efficiency of the work environment will be enhanced and God will be glorified.

> Jesus explained his style of leadership in relation to the self-seeking and domineering method of leadership that his followers were used to. James and John asked Jesus if

he would grant to them the privilege of sitting on his right and left in positions of leadership in his kingdom. But Jesus explained to them that their philosophy of leadership was not to be modeled after that of the "Gentiles" and "great men" of the world: "Whoever wants to be held in highest regard must be the servant of everyone else" (Mark 10:42–44; Matthew 20:25–28).[86]

Jesus clearly taught that leaders should adopt the attitude of servants (Luke 22:26). God has made it clear that He is not impressed by how many people serve you. Instead He commissions you to selflessly serve others—this is what He counts as greatness.

A leader who serves will continue to raise up more leaders who also serve. In that way, a culture of servant-leadership will be perpetuated. When Jesus washed the feet of His disciples (John 13), He made a bold statement about what servant-leadership looks like practically.

We learn from Jesus that servanthood is an overflow of an intimate relationship with God. Servant-leadership is not possible without the right mindset. You will not be able to lead others until you have learned to submit yourself to others.

Jesus was willing to serve the lowest of the low. He even wholeheartedly served the one who would betray Him (Judas). Ultimately, He gave His life for the sins of the whole world out of servant-hearted love. When He washed His disciples feet, He showed that even the greatest teacher should be willing to take the lowest place

Being a true servant-leader means that you have the character to serve without the motivation of selfish gain. Oftentimes, a leader will find their position requires more sacrifice than it does material gain. You need to be willing to give up your desires and to consider others more important than yourself.

Servant Leadership Is Not Weak[87]

Being a servant-leader doesn't just mean doing the things other people don't want to do, and at the same time it is not to be used to seek personal gain. A true servant-leader does everything they can to empower others. They are not above doing small thing, but they never lose sight of where they are going. Their primary motivation is pleasing God and not man:

> Am I now trying to win the approval of human beings, or of God? Or am I trying to please people? If I were still trying to please people, I would not be a servant of Christ. — Galatians 1:10 (NIV)

Servant-leadership is not an excuse to take a position of weakness or laziness. A key characteristic of a servant-leader is the ability to persevere when things are challenging. You should not allow others to take advantage of you because you are modeling servant-leadership. You still need to take a bold stand for what is honorable.

Personality Traits of a Servant-Leader[88]

One of the main characteristics of a servant-leader is their gracious and caring attitude. They don't think they're better than other people, and they aren't too proud to receive wisdom and help from others. They both lead and follow with humility.

Another primary characteristic of a servant-leader is their ability to empower others to be essential participants in accomplishing a mission. They are able to call out the good in others so they can rise to fulfill their full potential. An effective servant-leader invests in their followers so they can work together to accomplish their vision.

The greatness that a servant-leader strives for is in their ability to serve others. They walk with honor, sincerity, honesty, generosity, and humility. Their main goal is to see others raised up to walk in their gifting. A servant-leader selflessly sacrifices so that others can be blessed.

Servant-leaders still possess the ability to have strong direction and the ability to cast vision—but they carry out this vision by inviting others to be involved. At the same time, they "walk the talk" so that they're paving the way with their actions, not merely their words.

Something amazing about servant-leadership is that it provides you with the opportunity to be honest about your strengths and weaknesses. When you possess this information, you will be able to surround yourself with others who complement your abilities. This model will protect everyone from abusive power. It will allow every member of the team to play a vital role in fulfilling the vision.

Yet another essential characteristic of a servant-leader is the ability to be flexible in how situations are handled. Different situations may call for different actions, and a leader needs to discern which course of action will be best. In this way, they seek out what will work best to ensure the good of everyone.

The Benefits of the Servant-Leadership Style

A servant-leader seeks to put people before things. This leadership style can be applied to any organization or institution, and there are many benefits to the servant-leadership model.

First and foremost, servant-leaders benefit from having the attitude that Jesus had! Servant-leaders measure their success based on biblical principles and Kingdom values. Their timeline is submitted to God's timing, and they have eternity in view. They are more concerned with doing things the right way than merely getting ahead. A servant-leader finds value in others and includes them in their vision.[89]

Servant-leadership also benefits from the diversity of your team and organization as a whole. With servant-leadership, decisions aren't made by one person alone; instead, a diverse team of people contributes. Because servant-leaders care about what happens to others, they allow those who will be most impacted by a decision to be an influential part of making that decision.[90]

Diversity was originally God's idea, and was woven into the fabric of creation. He created male and female as the very first picture of diversity (Mark 10:6). God created even more diversity when He divided people by different languages at the Tower of Babel (Genesis 11:9). An organization will consist of different kinds of people with different backgrounds, ages, and cultures, but we are all united. Galatians 3:28 says, "There is neither Jew nor Gentile, neither slave nor free, nor is there male and female, for you are all one in Christ Jesus" (NIV).[91]

Every person's contribution is important because everybody plays a vital role for the ministry to be successful. A servant-leader therefore works to foster an environment that best serves each team member. In this type of model, the leader has the accessibility to interact personally with each team member— which works well when you have a diverse team. Servant-leadership works with diversity to help bring unity to the team.[92]

Servant leadership motivates everybody to get involved in the activities of the organization. Because every member is viewed as a valuable part of the team, they in turn feel free to participate. It helps alleviate people's fear of sharing their ideas.[93]

Ultimately, a servant leader encourages the gifts, talents, and skills in each team member. As a result, this model enables everyone to flourish, and the team can achieve the most optimal outcomes. When people see that their ideas are welcome and accepted, it encourages them to bring their best.[94]

In essence, servant-leadership is leading in the same way that Jesus led. This is true godly leadership. It is the kind of leadership that empowers others to do what they can to serve God and bring Him glory. It encourages a leader to lay down their life so that others may be blessed. This selfless leadership style enables people to live out a Christ-centered purpose.[95]

The priority of a servant-leader is to serve and honor Jesus Christ. As a result, they are not self-seeking, but rather are striving to serve Christ and others selflessly. Because a servant-leader is not seeking personal gain, they are not fearful about what will happen to them in their position. They are not afraid that someone will try to take their place or rise above them. A servant-leader is secure in Christ and truly wants to see everyone succeed.[96]

Do not be afraid, if you adopt a servant-leadership model, that your followers will not respect you because of your willingness to meet them on their level. To the contrary, when you are very close to the people you are leading, they will tell you more openly about what their ideas are. When we look at Jesus and His disciples, we see that they were very close to each other. The disciples were able to communicate freely with Jesus. He did not intimidate them with His position, but rather taught and trained them. Your followers will give you the highest respect if you approach them with love and humility.[97]

That said, those who serve in the Kingdom of God will have their character tested at every turn. A servant-leader must therefore welcome counsel, direction, and correction. As they allow themselves to by taught by God and experience, they will be strengthened in their innermost being. A servant-leader will grow in strength to persevere through any circumstance.[98]

LEADING TO GROW

Leadership is essential to a successful church or organization. There are many different attributes that makes someone a good leader. Even someone who is not a natural leader can learn to develop the skills to become an effective one.[99]

Every organization needs a leader who creates an inspiring vision for the future and motivates people to engage with that vision. When it comes to leadership, the corporate world is doing much better than churches. Churches are struggling to maintain good leaders because they primarily focus on the pastors and elders as leaders, and thereby limit the church's potential.

The Bible gives us many examples of leadership and how the church can be run efficiently. Romans 12 and 1 Corinthians 12 speak of unity—having many members all working together. We all know the importance of unity. However, it seems at times, we are more caught up in seeking our own desires than in trying to work together for the glory of God. Unity is a key ingredient for the success of most organizations, and it is just as essential for the church! The church needs to have leaders who will emphasize the importance of true unity.

Whether in a church or in another type of organization, people want to follow someone with a strong vision. They want to follow someone who knows where they are going and is worthy of respect. A leader who walks in integrity will find followers who are willing to trust them.[100]

As a Christian leader, you should follow scriptural wisdom for how to lead, rather than following the patterns of the world. You can seek out this wisdom and become a great leader even if you feel inadequate. Leadership can be learned if you devote yourself to doing whatever is necessary to grow. Areas you need help in can be delegated to others who are seeking to grow in leadership. No one can do everything alone, and allowing others to aide us will only increase our productivity. In this way, not only will you grow in leadership, but so will all of those who follow you.[101]

REFERENCES

1. Carr, Alan. "Sermons and Outlines: God's Answers for Man's Excuses." *Sermon Notebook*. **http://www.sermonnotebook.org/old%20testament/ex3_1-12.htm**
2. Newman, Willis and Esmie. "The Nature of Christian Leadership." *Bible-teaching-about.com*. Newman International. http://www.bible-teaching-about.com/Christianleadership.html
3. Krejcir, Richard. "What Is Leadership?" *ChurchLeaderhsip.org*. Institute of Church Leadership Development. http://www.churchleadership.org/apps/articles/?articleid=65616&columnid=4541&contentonly=true
4. Faulkner, Brooks. "Seven Models of Biblical Leadership." *Lifeway*. LifeWay Christian Resources. http://www.lifeway.com/Article/church-leadership-seven-biblical-models
5. "Biblical Leadership." *ChurchLeaderhsip.org*. Institute of Church Leadership Development. http://www.churchleadership.org/pages.asp?pageid=66921

6. "1 Timothy 4:12" From Charles J. Ellicot, "Ellicot's Commentary for English Readers." *BibleHub*. http://biblehub.com/commentaries/1_timothy/4-12.htm
7. Gill, John. "Commentary on Titus 2:7." *The New John Gill Exposition of the Entire Bible*. 1999. www.studylight.org/commentaries/geb/titus-2.html
8. Krejcir, Richard. "Fruit of the Spirit Is Love." *Discipleship Tools*. Into Thy Word. http://www.discipleshiptools.org/apps/articles/default.asp?articleid=36685&columnid=4166
9. "Mission Statement versus Vision Statement." *Diffen*. http://www.diffen.com/difference/Mission_Statement_vs_Vision_Statement
10. *Ibid*.
11. Malphurs, Aubrey. "Developing a Vision." From *Advanced Strategic Planning*. Baker Books, 1999. http://hillconsultinggroup.org/assets/pdfs/articles/dev-vision.pdf
12. *Ibid*.
13. "Mission Statement versus Vision Statement." *Diffen*. http://www.diffen.com/difference/Mission_Statement_vs_Vision_Statement
14. "The Mission of the Church." *Church of Christ*. https://www.newtestamentchurch.org/html/Elmore/mission_of_the_church.htm
15. Distelzweig, Howard. Scott B. Droege (ed.). "Organizational Structure." *Reference for Business*. Advameg Inc.

http://www.referenceforbusiness.com/management/Ob-Or/Organizational-Structure.html
16. "What Is a Prophet/Prophetess?" *Truth or Tradition?* Spirit and Truth Fellowship International. From *Prophecy: Understanding and Utilizing the Manifestation of Prophecy.* http://www.truthortradition.com/articles/what-is-a-prophet-prophetess
17. *Ibid.*
18. "Doctrine of the Pastor-Teacher." Makarios Bible Church. http://makarios-online.org/notes/doctrine/Pastor-teacher%206-06.doc
19. Hoelscher, Timothy. "The Role of the Pastor-Teacher in the Local Church." *GraceTeaching.com.*
20. "The Apostles." *InSearchOfTruth.org.* http://www.insearchoftruth.org/articles/apostles.html
21. "The Office of the Apostle Explained." *HubPages.* http://hubpages.com/religion-philosophy/The-Office-of-the-Apostle-Explained
22. *Ibid.*
23. Murphy, Richard A. *Reforming the Leadership of the Church.*
24. *Ibid.*
25. *Ibid.*
26. Davison, Roy. "The Work of an Evangelist. Old Paths Archive. From lecture at Peterborough, England, August 1986. http://oldpaths.com/Archive/Davison/Roy/Allen/1940/workevan.html

27. "Evangelist." *Easton's Bible Dictionary.* In *Bible Study Tools.* http://www.biblestudytools.com/dictionaries/eastons-bible-dictionary/evangelist.html
28. "Evangelist." *Smith's Bible Dictionary.* In *Bible Study Tools.* http://www.biblestudytools.com/dictionaries/smiths-bible-dictionary/evangelist.html
29. "What Does the Bible Say about Christian Character?" *GotQuestions.org.* Got Questions Ministries. http://www.gotquestions.org/Christian-character.html
30. Krejcir, Richard J. "The Character of Discipline." *Discipleship Tools.* Into Thy Word. http://www.discipleshiptools.org/apps/articles/?articleid=37154&columnid=4166. From *ChurchLeadership.org.*
31. Krejcir, Richard J. "The Character of Integrity." *Discipleship Tools.* Into Thy Word. http://www.churchleadership.org/apps/articles/?articleid=42531&columnid=4542. From *ChurchLeadership.org.*
32. Krejcir, Richard J. "What Is Obedience?" *Discipleship Tools.* Into Thy Word. http://www.discipleshiptools.org/apps/articles/default.asp?articleid=39847&columnid=. From *ChurchLeadership.org.*
33. Clark, C. S. "60 Character Traits of Christ." *Seek This Jesus.* http://seekthisjesus.com/60-character-traits-of-christ
34. Krejcir, Richard J. "The Character of Gratitude." *Discipleship Tools.* Into Thy Word. http://www.discipleshiptools.org/apps/articles/?articleid=37105&columnid=4166. From *ChurchLeadership.org.*

35. Krejcir, Richard J. "The Character of Appreciation." *Discipleship Tools*. Into Thy Word. http://www.discipleshiptools.org/apps/articles/?articleid=37155&columnid=4166. From *ChurchLeadership.org*.
36. Murray, David. "The Most Essential Life Skill: Teachability." *Head Heart Hand Blog*. http://headhearthand.org/blog/2013/03/04/the-most-essential-life-skill-teachability/
37. Maxwell, John. In "A Teachable Spirit" by user 'Lyli.' *3-D Lessons for Life*. 4 March 2015. http://3dlessons4life.com/a-teachable-spirit/
38. Krejcir, Richard J. "The Character of Discernment." *Discipleship Tools*. Into Thy Word. http://www.discipleshiptools.org/apps/articles/default.asp?articleid=37128&columnid=4166. From *ChurchLeadership.org*.
39. Krejcir, Richard J. "The Character of Tolerance." *Discipleship Tools*. Into Thy Word. http://www.discipleshiptools.org/apps/articles/?articleid=37129&columnid=4166. From *ChurchLeadership.org*.
40. Krejcir, Richard J. "The Character of Humility." *Discipleship Tools*. Into Thy Word. http://www.discipleshiptools.org/apps/articles/?articleid=37101&columnid=4166. From *ChurchLeadership.org*.
41. Krejcir, Richard J. "The Character of Fairness." *Discipleship Tools*. Into Thy Word. http://www.discipleshiptools.org/apps/articles/?articleid=37136&columnid=4166. From *ChurchLeadership.org*.

42. Krejcir, Richard J. "The Character of Friendship." *Discipleship Tools*. Into Thy Word. http://www.discipleshiptools.org/apps/articles/?articleid=37137&columnid=4166. From *ChurchLeadership.org*.
43. Krejcir, Richard J. "The Character of Efficiency." *Discipleship Tools*. Into Thy Word. http://www.discipleshiptools.org/apps/articles/?articleid=37146&columnid=4166. From *ChurchLeadership.org*.
44. Krejcir, Richard. "The Character of Encouragement." *Into Thy Word*. Into Thy Word Ministries. http://www.intothyword.org/apps/articles/?articleid=35199&contentonly=true
45. Krejcir, Richard. "The Character of Punctuality." *Discipleship Tools*. Into Thy Word. http://www.discipleshiptools.org/apps/articles/?articleid=37122&columnid=4166. From *ChurchLeadership.org*.
46. Krejcir, Richard. "The Character of Attentiveness." *Into Thy Word*. Into Thy Word Ministries. http://www.intothyword.org/apps/articles/?articleid=35201&columnid=3803
47. Krejcir, Richard. "The Character of Compassion." *Into Thy Word*. Into Thy Word Ministries. http://www.intothyword.org/apps/articles/default.asp?blogid=3803%20&view=post&articleid=35204&fldKeywords=&fldAuthor=&fldTopic=0
48. Krejcir, Richard. "The Character of Flexibility." *Discipleship Tools*. Into Thy Word. http://www.discipleshiptools.org/apps/articles/?articleid=37152&columnid=4166. From *ChurchLeadership.org*.

49. Krejcir, Richard. "The Character of Boldness." *Discipleship Tools*. Into Thy Word. http://www.discipleshiptools.org/apps/articles/?articleid=37121&columnid=4166. From *ChurchLeadership.org*.
50. Clark, C. S. "60 Character Traits of Christ." *Seek This Jesus*. http://seekthisjesus.com/60-character-traits-of-christ
51. Downing, Jim. "Importance of the Word of God." *Discipleship Library*. http://www.discipleshiplibrary.com
52. "An Inspiring Introduction to the Holy Book." *The Gideons International*. http://blog.gideons.org/2010/12/the-bible-contains-the-mind-of-god/
53. Wellman, Jack. "How Do I Meditate on the Word of God? Good Bible Tips." *What Christians Want to Know*. Telling Ministries LLC. http://www.whatchristianswanttoknow.com/how-do-i-meditate-on-the-word-of-god-good-bible-tips/
54. "Regurgitate." *Merriam-Webster*. http://www.merriam-webster.com/dictionary/regurgitate
55. Wellman, Jack. "How Do I Meditate on the Word of God? Good Bible Tips." *What Christians Want to Know*. Telling Ministries LLC. http://www.whatchristianswanttoknow.com/how-do-i-meditate-on-the-word-of-god-good-bible-tips/
56. MacArthur, John. "Why Is It Important for me to Study the Bible? (2 Timothy 3:16–7)" *Grace to You*. https://www.gty.org/resources/questions/QA168/Why-is-it-important-for-me-to-study-the-Bible
57. *Ibid*.
58. *Ibid*.

59. *Ibid.*
60. *Ibid.*
61. *Ibid.*
62. *Ibid.*
63. *Ibid.*
64. Pete, Reve' M. "The Importance of the Word of God." *A Fresh Start Online.* Reve' M. Pete Ministries Inc. http://revempete.us/inspirational/importantword.html
65. *Ibid.*
66. *Ibid.*
67. "What the Bible Says about Prayer." *Just Pray.* http://www.justpray.org/BiblicalPrayer.html
68. Edmonson, Ron. "7 Sure Ways to Grow as a Leader." *Ron Edmonson.* http://www.ronedmondson.com/2013/10/7-sure-ways-grow-leader.html
69. Hutton, Laura. "Why Teamwork Is Important in the Workplace." *Official Blog.* Australian Institute of Business. http://aib.edu.au/blog/teamwork-is-important-in-the-workplace/
70. Krejcir, Richard J. "The Character of Efficiency." *Discipleship Tools.* Into Thy Word. http://www.discipleshiptools.org/apps/articles/?articleid=37146&columnid=4166. From *ChurchLeadership.org.*
71. Hutton, Laura. "Why Teamwork Is Important in the Workplace." *Official Blog.* Australian Institute of Business. http://aib.edu.au/blog/teamwork-is-important-in-the-workplace/
72. *Ibid.*
73. *Ibid.*

74. *Ibid.*
75. *Ibid.*
76. "Teamwork." *GotQuestions.org.* Got Questions Ministries. https://www.gotquestions.org/Bible-teamwork.html
77. *Ibid.*
78. "Core Values: Servant Leadership as a Way of Life." From *TWU Core Values Statement Series No. 3*. Trinity Western University. 5 Feb. 2000. http://www.twu.ca/about/values/servant-leadership-life.html
79. *Ibid.*
80. *Ibid.*
81. *Ibid.*
82. "What the Bible Says about Teamwork." *Bridge to the Bible*. Syndey Christadelphian Ecclesia Incorporated. http://www.bridgetothebible.com/What%20does%20Bible%20say/35%20Teamwork.htm
83. *Ibid.*
84. *Ibid.*
85. *Ibid.*
86. *Ibid.*
87. *Ibid.*
88. *Ibid.*
89. Ricciardelli, Robert. "A True Servant Leader Does All Things for God's Glory." *Ministry Today Magazine*. http://ministrytodaymag.com/index.php/pastors-heart/19646-a-true-servant-leader-does-all-things-for-god-s-glory

90. Root, George N., III. "The Advantages of the Servant Leadership Style." *Chron*. Hearst Newspapers LLC. http://smallbusiness.chron.com/advantages-servant-leadership-style-11693.html
91. "What Does the Bible Say about Diversity?" *GotQuestions.org*. Got Questions Ministries. https://www.gotquestions.org/Bible-diversity.html
92. Root, George N., III. "The Advantages of the Servant Leadership Style." *Chron*. Hearst Newspapers LLC. http://smallbusiness.chron.com/advantages-servant-leadership-style-11693.html
93. *Ibid.*
94. O'Dwyer, Gemma. "Advantages and Disadvantages of Servant Leadership in Education." *Ms. O'Dwyer's College Blog*. 21 Jan. 2014. https://5j2014msodwyer.wordpress.com/2014/01/21/advantages-and-disadvantages-of-servant-leadership-in-education/
95. Krejcir, Richard J. "Servant Leadership Principles." *ChurchLeadership.org*. http://www.churchleadership.org/apps/articles/?articleid=41928&columnid=4540
96. *Ibid.*
97. *Ibid.*
98. *Ibid.*
99. Curry, Myron. "Leadership: What Makes a Good Leader." *Business Training Media*. http://www.businesstrainingmedia.com/article-leaders.php

100. "Concepts of Leadership." *Big Dog & Little Dog's Performance Juxtaposition.*
 http://www.nwlink.com/~donclark/leader/leadcon.html
101. *Ibid.*
102. Krejcir, Richard J. "Servant Leadership Checklist." *ChurchLeadership.org.*
 http://www.churchleadership.org/apps/articles/default.asp?articleid=41927&columnid=454

APPENDIX
Complementary Discussion Questions[102]

It is important as a leader to evaluate yourself regularly to see if you are being the kind of leader that God calls you to be. You have to check your motives and make sure you are leading with the right heart and for the right reasons. Are you being the kind of leader who reflects God's heart?

As godly leaders we must submit our desires to God, and obey His guidance. If we are truly leading like Christ, we are empowering others to do the work of God as well (Philippians 3:10–17; 1 Timothy 4:11–14; 2 Timothy 2:15; Titus 2:6–8).

Leaders should ask themselves:

- Do I have clear goals and biblical purpose as a leader, or are my motivations and objectives personal? Do my goals include spiritual growth?
- Do my leadership team and membership known and understand the vision and mission of our organization?
- Am I equipping others to live out God's purposes for them? Are they competent in the skills, habits, and characteristics they need? Do they have the resources they need for success?
- Do I acknowledge, love, and appreciate people who are

working hard or being good examples?
- Do I address conflicts and offenses in a firm but friendly way?
- Does my team trust me and know I care?
- Do I provide feedback to my team members? Do they feel free to offer feedback to me?
- Does my team focus on prayer?
- Do the people on my team and in my organization build on each other's strengths and support each other?

You should make it your priority to care about the needs of those in your care, and you ought to be willing to hear what they have to contribute. As you respect your team members, you will foster an atmosphere of respect that is shared by all.

As a leader you are first and foremost a servant of Christ, and it is your responsibility to be an example of what that looks like. You are called to lead your followers in alignment with God's heart for them!

About the Author

Meet RICHMOND DONKOR

Richmond is Author, songwriter, singer, self-development coach, Evangelist, Pastor, teacher, motivational speaker and philanthropist. He is the author of 3 steps to Overcome Poverty, The Call With Promise; From wretch to Riches, How to Evangelize With Confidence, The Ultimate Wife, The Ultimate Husband, The Ultimate Dream Family and Created to Lead. Richmond has been preaching, teaching, training, and planting churches in South-East Asia and currently he is the associate pastor at the Restored House Chapel Ministries in Vancouver, Canada. He enjoys reading, writing, praying, and singing praises and worship songs. Learn more about him from his website: http://www.evangelistrichmond.com/

1. THE CALL WITH PROMISE

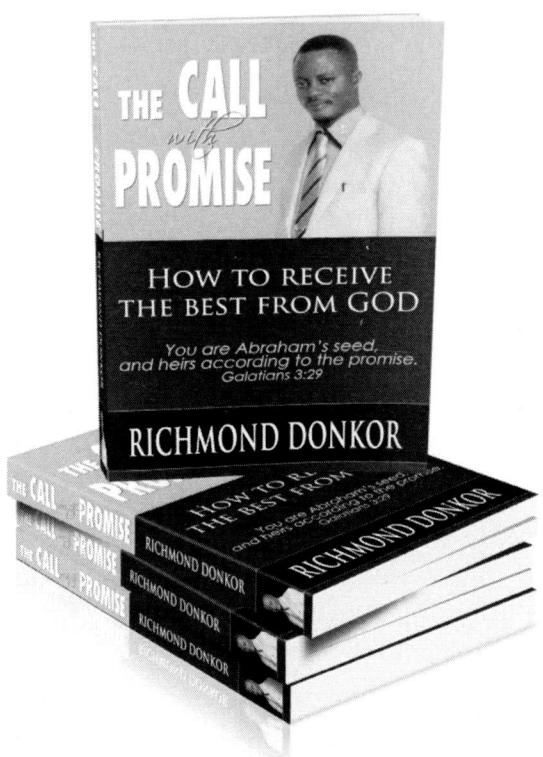

No matter how old you are, where you're from or what you do for a living, we all share something in common—a desire to be successful. The question most of us ask ourselves is what can I do to become more successful? How can I excel in all areas of life, whether in your spirituality, family, career, business, and education? We were miss-informed by well-meaning people and institutions that told us that success is hard to come by, a struggle. You probably mistakenly believe that you are not good enough, smart enough, etc. These beliefs are just lies you have told yourself that you have come to believe. The fact is that you have everything you need inside of you right now to become a huge success. The challenge is to excavate your treasure and bring it to the light so that everyone can see and appreciate who you are and what you can do. The treasure that is within you are your God-given gifts, as well as having the ability to trust in a higher power who wants you to be healthy, wealthy, and wise. There are a lot of steps that you can use to be more successful if we know how to set clear intentions, apply focused attention, and take massive action daily. Always remember the essential Truth that you already have all that you need to attract more success and happiness, you just need to learn to access your inner power. This is what The Call with Promise book is about. Learn secrete you have never heard before in your life to unleash the power within you and build a successful life that you deserve. These truths have changed my life and I strongly believe that it will open your inner eyes and ears for you to build a huge success in all aspect of your life.

2. THE ULTIMATE HUSBAND

How do you know if a man is a player or a keeper? How do you know if a man you are dating is a potential husband? What makes a man a dream husband? Is it his appearance, his Career, his wealth, his fame, his spiritual life, his Social life, and his talents? People often ask me why divorce has become so prevalent in our society. Many people enter into marriage without realizing how complex marriage is. Proper preparation is crucial. Preparing doesn't guarantee everything will go exactly as we plan, but it gives us an awareness of potential blessings and dangers we may encounter in marriage. Preparation is crucial to everything we do in life and generally leads to a stronger performance. The reason why many relationships suffer unnecessarily is because of a poorly laid foundation. Much of the preparation that precedes today's marriages relates to the wedding and other transitory matters unrelated to the growth and maintenance of a healthy, lasting relationship. There are countless things that should be considered before marriage. Women frequently say they can't find a man who will truly love and understand them. The best things in life rarely come easily, and finding a good husband is definitely a challenge. You must take the time to prepare yourself to meet the right man to become your husband—a man who will care for you throughout the rest of your life. Without good direction and proper preparation, you may end up with the wrong man and an unhappy marriage. You must also remember that both the man and the woman should be committed to building a successful family. You have a huge part to play in the success of your marriage as well. Why do you want to get married? Here are some important questions to ask yourself and answer sincerely:

- Is it because of the pressure from your family or friends?
- Is it because all of your friends are married and you are lonely?
- Is it because you want to have children and you're getting older?
- Is it because a man has helped you, so you want to marry him out of gratitude or as a kindness?
- Is it because you don't want to lose him?
- Is it to gain financial security?
- Is it because you are pregnant with his child?
- Is it to avoid the temptation of premarital sex?
- Is it because other men are coming on to you?
- Is it because he is the best-looking guy you have ever met?

- Is it because he is intelligent, talented, famous, or from a respected family?
- Is it because you are prepared and ready spiritually, socially, economically, and emotionally to start a family? I do believe that The Ultimate Husband book will help you to make a great decision in choosing your life partner.

3. THE ULTIMATE WIFE

What makes a woman a dream wife? Is it her appearance, her Career, her wealth, her fame, her spiritual life, her Social life, and her talents? I do believe with all my heart that every woman can be a dream wife. Men and women who marry usually love each other deeply, but that love too often transforms into anger and frustration, which leads in turn to separation and divorce. In such cases, something in the relationship was amiss—some problem that ought to have been prevented or addressed in order to establish a happy home.

If God leads you down the path of marriage, however, then you must approach the matter in all seriousness. Finding and choosing the person who will complete your life, and joining that person in holy matrimony, is no trifling affair; it requires preparation and direction. Entering into a marriage is like starting a lifelong journey. To successfully face challenges, reach your intended destinations, and enjoy the many other experiences that you will share along the way, you need spiritual, emotional, psychological, physical, and material preparation.

Whether you are married yet or not, this book will help women to understand how to be good wives—and men to be good husbands. Husbands and wives alike should also pray for each other to be good spouses. Of course, if you are currently unmarried, this book will better prepare and enable you to find the ultimate wife—your dream wife.

4. THE ULTIMATE FAMILY

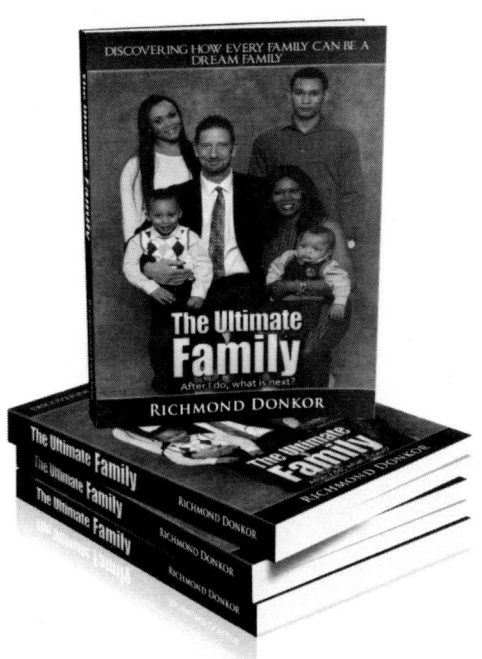

Are you happy in your marriage life? If you are happy, do you want to take your marriage into the highest happiest level? This book will help you to understand the secret behind every happy family. It is also good for pastors and marriage counselors for pre and post marital counseling. Adam praised Eve when he first saw her; but when troubles came, he blamed God for giving her to him. In Genesis 3:12 Adam said, "The woman whom you gave to be with me, she gave me fruit of the tree, and I ate" (ESV). This was the first ever-marital disagreement—but notice that Adam did not ask for divorce as we often do today. Adam and Eve were the first people to get married.

They had everything they needed in order to enjoy their marriage, but they still experienced misunderstandings and disagreements—even though their circumstances were perfect and there wasn't any sin. We don't pray for problems, but problems are inevitable. Each family faces different challenges, and most of these challenges have the ability to end marriages. There is no doubt that Satan and his angels are fighting against families. However, I believe there are some important principles that most families do not apply properly—principles that would allow them to stand strong against Satan. The book addresses major family problems in our modern days. Have you ever heard a statement " No money no honey? Well today, the problems families are facing does not limit to money alone. There is money but no honey. If you want to bring honey to your marriage, I strongly recommend this book. You need to read Ultimate Husband and Ultimate Wife to fully understand what it takes to be a wonderful husband and wife.

5. HOW TO EVANGELIZE WITH CONFIDENCE

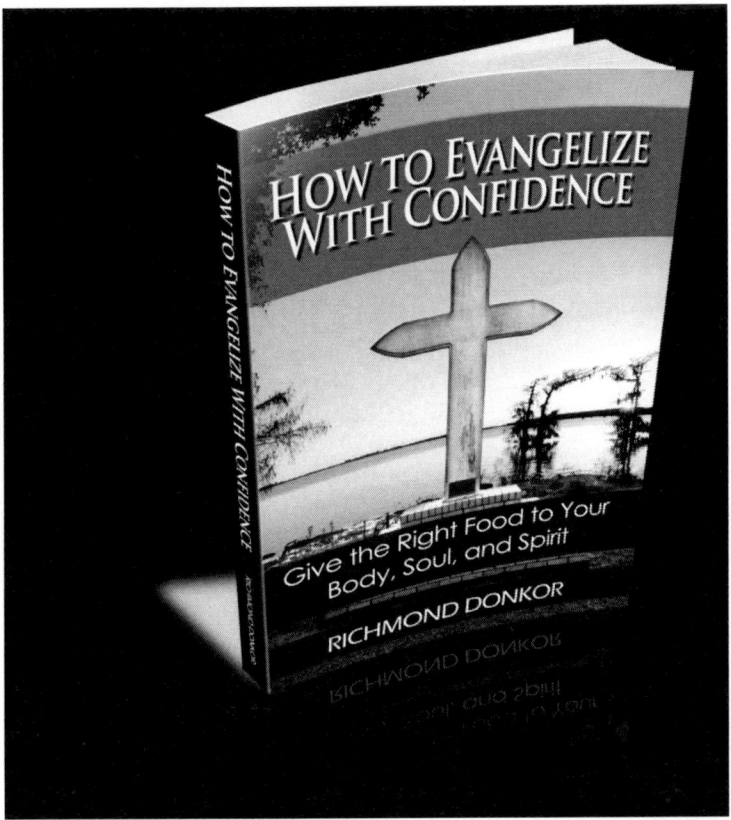

Evangelism is very important to every ministry, but unfortunately, it has become a challenge for churches and individuals alike nowadays. I hear people say that they don't know how to evangelize; they don't know where or how to start a conversation about Jesus. Jesus always sought other people out to evangelize to them. He went to their workplaces and homes, showing concern for them and sharing fellowship with them. As Paul wrote to the Romans: For "Everyone who calls on the name of the LORD will be saved." 14 But how can they call on him to save them unless they believe in him? And how can they believe in him if they have never heard about him? And how can they hear about him unless someone tells them? 15 And how will anyone go and tell them without being sent? That is why the Scriptures say, "How beautiful are the feet of the messengers who bring good news!" (Romans 10:13-15 NLT) People are suffering and seriously searching for solutions to their problems. Though not everyone will accept the truth, if we do not at least make the effort to tell them, then we will never know who might accept Jesus and who will reject Him. Our responsibility is to let people know what will help them to overcome the challenges they are facing in life. It is vital for every believer to learn how to evangelize and win souls for Christ, for He is coming soon This book will help you to present the gospel with a confidence to anyone.

Created to Lead

6. GODIVA—FROM WRETCH TO RICHES

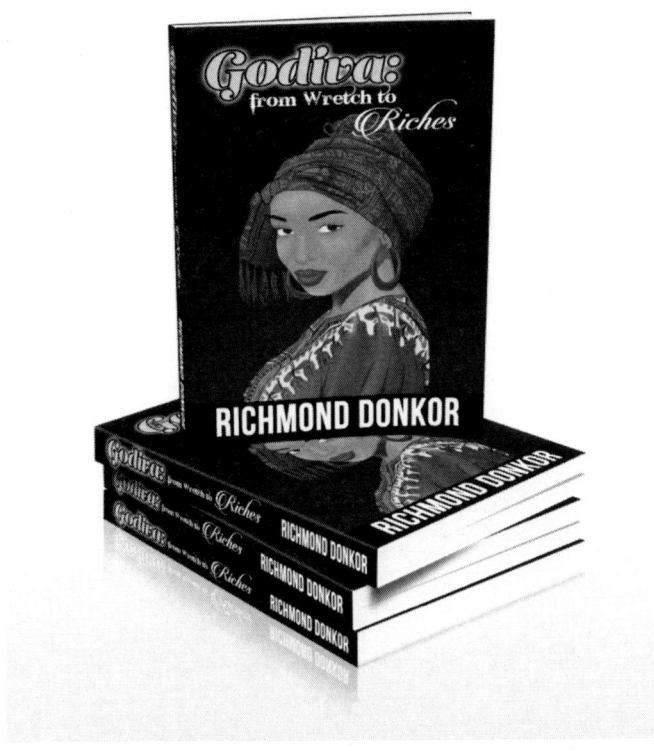

This is one of the most powerful and interesting stories I have heard. Godiva started life well but went on to fail miserably. She threw away her two sons after giving birth to them, and she involved herself in many many practices. She became hopeless because failure was following her everywhere she went. Her own parents and best friends left her when she was desperately in need. But her failure turned to success because of some things that she eventually realized about herself. Her life changed completely. Meanwhile, those children she had thrown away became successful people. She said "failure is inevitable in life; but if we know how to handle it, we can easily turn it to success"

Does failure have a significant impact in our lives? Have you ever asked yourself where failure comes from? Are you tired of constantly failing? Do you know that your failure could be turned to success? Failure is the best teacher in life, and anyone who wants to taste success must pass through its hands.

Perhaps you have failed in your marriage, your job, or your business; and because of that, you have given up. Remember, failure becomes defeat only when you give up. Your failure in life does not make you the worst person in this world, but it makes you an experienced person in life. Every successful person fails at some point—and usually many times—but refuses to give up. Failure tells you about your weaknesses, shortcomings, insufficient preparations, and insufficient efforts. Facing failure can make you stronger, wiser, and more resolute, and can spur you on to greatest efforts.

Failures are the stepping stones to success—as long as you analyze your mistakes and then try again, applying what you've learned. Therefore, if you can manage to learn from failures, you will eventually reach your intended destination. Making a mistake is not a crime; rather, the ability to learn from mistakes contributes to lasting success. If you are planning to quit, it will give you a great reason why you should not give up your dreams. This story will help you to stand up again if you are down. I don't know what you are going through in life, but one thing I want to assure you is that this story will change your life for good.

Where to buy all these books:

Both printed and ebook:
Amazon: amazon.com/author/richmonddonkor

Website: evangelistrichmond.com/

Facebook: evangelistdonkor

Twitter: richkobbs

Richmond Donkor